The Story of
PRIVATE SECURITY

The Story of

PRIVATE SECURITY

By

JOHN DONALD PEEL

CHARLES C THOMAS · PUBLISHER
Springfield · Illinois · U.S.A.

Published and Distributed Throughout the World by
CHARLES C THOMAS • PUBLISHER
BANNERSTONE HOUSE
301-327 East Lawrence Avenue, Springfield, Illinois, U.S.A.
NATCHEZ PLANTATION HOUSE
735 North Atlantic Boulevard, Fort Lauderdale, Florida, U.S.A.

With THOMAS BOOKS *careful attention is given to all details of manufacturing and design. It is the Publisher's desire to present books that are satisfactory as to their physical qualities and artistic possibilities and appropriate for their particular use.* THOMAS BOOKS *will be true to those laws of quality that assure a good name and good will.*

Printed in the United States of America
N-1

This book is dedicated to my wife

Foreword

THIS BOOK offers historical and vocational information about the privately licensed security officer (the modern successor to the old-time watchman) and his work.

Security officers are today indispensable to industrial and commercial undertakings. By protecting plants and stores and factories and warehouses, and the employees and equipment and supplies in them, security officers enable business enterprises to operate in a safe and orderly manner, to provide jobs for millions of workers, and to make a fair profit.

For years they have quietly done their job without much notice or encouragement, their solitary patrol unmarked as often as not even by the employers who hired their services, and suddenly there has come to pass a sociological climate in which they are in the spotlight.

In these pages you will learn much about these men and women (widely known as security officers, though across the nation their titles are as variable as the weather) who engage in supplementary law enforcement work in support of the local police officers. Hired and paid by private employers, their authority and powers are defined by statute and they usually work at a basic level of law enforcement.

Since this is the level where some observers see the police on the defensive today, stemming the criminal tide with incredible courage and resourcefulness but harassed and badgered and beset, capable and devoted security officers are becoming recognized as an expedient for any community and a resource for any police department.

After all, police departments and welfare bureaus are not the only ones involved with unemployment, mental illness, racism, poverty, dissension, and the problems they spawn. The men and women in private security face such facts of life each day and, more image-conscious now than ever before, they are trying valiantly to live up to their potential and to grow in law enforcement stature.

Temporarily they lack many things—uniform standards of qualification and performance, public recognition and acceptance, job training and security, to name a few—but the situation is swiftly changing under the pressures of the day.

Naturally the views and opinions expressed throughout this book are those of the author and do not necessarily represent the views of any police department or security agency. They are proffered in the modest hope that some readers may find them reasonable and acceptable, and may be moved to enter this field of law enforcement, make of it a lifetime career, and help to hasten the improvements that are building. At the very least, a better understanding of this hitherto somewhat neglected law enforcement resource may result.

In the interest of clarity it should be understood that in these pages we are not discussing the private detective or private investigator, who is a different sort of person bringing different talents to a different kind of job. Nor are we talking about the jail or prison guard whose work, though critically important, does not always match that of a security officer as defined herein.

Any resemblance to persons living or dead of characters created for illustrative purposes in these pages is, of course, purely coincidental.

Saint Louis, Missouri   J.D.P.

Contents

The Story of
PRIVATE SECURITY

I
THE PAST

In The Beginning

Long Ago and Far Away

SOME FORM of law, and some form of enforcement, whether imposed by church or state, can be traced back to civilizations now dust a thousand years.

From her beginnings in the Nile Valley 4000 years before the birth of Christ, Egypt knew the trials of law enforcement.

The empires of the Chinese, the Greeks, the Hebrews, the Persians, and the Romans all faced comparable problems.

Traces of primitive law and primitive enforcement remain from all these cultures, as well as the ones which followed (or continued) in the Christian era; so too do scraps of information about the police bodies that supported the laws of the times. Such traces persist despite the erosion of time and the destruction of irreplaceable records by fire and flood and vandalism.

There are not, of course, any such traces in those parts of the world where crime was considered a personal matter to be canceled by the victim or his family through vendetta or death feud or clan vengeance.

The watchman was known in Old Testament times* and over the years has often been the citizens' only protection.

Law enforcement has frequently appeared to be a military undertaking because it made use of the troops or military bodyguards that protected the ruling families of the time. Guards (or *guardsmen*) were the picked soldiers who comprised the house-

---

*Psalm 127. Except the LORD build the house, they labour in vain that build it; except the LORD keep the city, the watchman waketh *but* in vain.

Isaiah xxi:6. For thus hath the LORD said unto me, Go, set a watchman, let him declare what he seeth.

Ezekiel xxxiii:6. But if the watchman see the sword come, and blow not the trumpet, and the people be not warned; if the sword come and take *any* person from among them, he is taken away in his iniquity; but his blood will I require at the watchman's hand.

hold troops assigned to royal families. Examples of such guardsmen, who commonly received special privileges in pay, promotions, and working conditions, would be the Praetorian guards of
ancient Rome or the Mamelukes of Egypt. Such guard units generally ceased to exist when their government changed form from
monarchy, and those which remain are mostly ceremonial troops,
as for example the Swiss Guards at the Vatican. Not entirely,
however: Great Britain still has a number of guard regiments.

The policing and patrolling practices of our own country
came from England, and it is to England that we must look for
information about our law enforcement beginnings.

The Anglo-Saxon System

When the Anglo-Saxons* settled in England about 400 A.D.,
they brought with them a system of compulsory communal responsibility for taking care of the law enforcement in, and the
military protection of, the family, the tribe, and the village.

The system organized the people into groups of ten families
or householders, called a *tithing* (from the Old English *teogotha:*
tenth) , and further into groups of ten *tithings* (that is, ten tens)
called a *hundred.* These groups, with some variations, were responsible for the behavior and safety of their members. Each man
was indeed his brother's keeper.

The *tithing* (initially the basic group of ten families or householders in a community and later also a geographical division to
which the system gave its name) selected a *tithingman*—a ruler of
ten—to represent the members. The ten tithingmen (representing
a *hundred,* of course, or ten groups of ten) had a king's *reeve* to
speak for them. Several *hundreds* made up a *shire* (an administrative district made up of the *hundreds* which united for mutual
protection and government control) and a *shire reeve* (from
which the word *sheriff* comes) was their spokesman to the king.

---

*A name given to German-speaking people who settled in England at the end of
Roman rule. The Angles (probably from Schleswig) and the Saxons settled in
England about the same time. The Jutes, from around the mouth of the Rhine
River, also came to England, and in the sixteenth century the term Anglo-Saxon
began to be used to denote non-Celtic settlers in England. Today the term is more
loosely used to denote any peoples (or their descendants) of the British Isles, including Danes and Normans.

A *shire reeve* could command the support of the entire *shire* in any case of need. Such need might be a matter of common defense, or the hunting down of a criminal. In such instances the *reeve* could assemble the strength of the *tithings* and the *hundreds* in a common venture of military enterprise or law enforcement.

The protection of law-abiding citizens and enforcement of the laws of the tribe or the community lay in the hands of the tribe or community.

The members of the groups were themselves responsible for whatever offenses were committed within their borders. They were required to capture, or surrender, the wrongdoer or make good the damage done and pay a fine.

And if you, being modern and practical, wonder if anybody would really hunt down or turn in a member of his own village or group, the indications are that the procedure worked pretty well.

These simple folk—simple in our sophisticated view, at least —were not so obsessed by the "rights" of criminals as we are today. They believed that the criminal had some responsibilities along with his rights; and that if he chose to ignore his responsibilities and prey on society, the choice was indeed his to make. However, he could not have it both ways. If he chose to make war on the law-abiding, he thereby sacrificed the privileges of the law-abiding; and when he was caught, he was fined or mutilated or killed.

Law enforcement was anchored firmly to a pair of simple beliefs:

First, it was considered the duty of every citizen to be a policeman whenever the need arose; second, it was considered that the lawbreaker, by his disregard for the rights of everybody except himself, could reasonably expect no more consideration than he gave.

By our standards today, these people were probably ignorant, superstitious, and gullible; but they possessed a basic honesty and a basic shrewdness which unwaveringly regarded right as being good and wrong as being bad, insofar as they could identify right and wrong. There were very few gray areas in their concepts.

Life at its best was hard enough and they had little time or energy to waste on a thief or a murderer. They were little concerned about the rights of a criminal who had already callously denied rights to the victim.

The people never blamed a skunk for stinking, but neither did they feel obligated to bring the beast into their homes to be rehabilitated. The discovered criminal was removed from society as immediately, directly, and permanently as a poisonous snake was removed from a house, and whatever sympathy and help were available went to the victims.

The *tithingman,* and from about the year 1100 the *constable,* was the official unpaid guardian of the community.

The *constable* (both the title and the office) was introduced into England by the Normans in 1066. The word comes from the late Latin *comes stabuli,* meaning an officer of the stable, a chief equerry, a head groom. This man was an officer of the household of the early English kings and over the years rose in importance to a position where he commanded the king's armies in the absence of the monarch. A *constable* was appointed to every *hundred* and was responsible for suppressing violent crimes and riots.

In the city, the constable was Captain of the Watch (or Chief of Police), responsible for overseeing the watchmen and for keeping the peace. As can be seen, this man had little in common with the police officer who later came to be called "constable." The early English constable's duties were administrative, legal, and executive, concerned with court functions and city affairs. County affairs were the concern of the sheriff. The title was abolished in 1872 except as it was incorporated into the County Police System.

In the United States, elimination of the office of constable began as early as 1830, and where it was retained, the officer began to lose his authority in criminal matters and became chiefly concerned with the issuing of writs and processes and election notices.

The Waits

Waits (or *waytes*) were known in England at least from 1200 A.D., first as municipal watchmen and later as official street musicians. They endured for several hundred shadowy years and very little documented information remains concerning them.

There are records of *waits* (that is, persons who watch or wait; watchmen; sentinels) at Norwich in 1288 and in Exeter in 1396. Sir Thomas Malory, who wrote *The Death of Arthur* about 1470, could say: "At last by fortune he came to a Castel and there he herd the waytes vpon the wallys."

The language of the day, now mostly obsolete, reflected the title. For example, *to make wait* meant "to keep watch"; *to have in wait* meant "to keep under observation"; *to lay good wait* meant "to be carefully on the watch." Even today we say that a criminal "lies in wait" for a victim.

Landowners apparently paid the sheriff an annual wait-fee (evidently computed on the size of the tax the landowner paid to the king) for the services of these watchmen who—among their duties—blew some type of horn or trumpet at three specified hours of the night in summer and at four specified hours of the night in winter as a signal of assurance. Since the waits did not all use the same type of instrument, the notes they blew did not have the same pitch. From such a beginning, and by slow degrees (and all too probably because of the need to add a bit of income to the miserable stipend they received), the waits evolved into groups of strolling minstrels or public musicians even while they were continuing their original watchman functions.

The waits were watchmen at least into the 1500's and continued as musicians until about 1800.

In 1285 (the thirteenth year of the reign of King Edward I) the Statute of Winchester, one of history's lawmaking landmarks,* appointed two constables to be chosen in every *hundred,* and established among its law enforcement provisions a regular system of night patrols in the towns.

Patrol was considered an affair of the night (there was none such during the daytime), needed in the dark hours to take care of the settlement and its people. So the men, particularly those

---

*The Statute really contained little that was new; rather, it set down all the workable law enforcement experience which had been distilled from years of trial and error.

between sixteen and twenty-one, who might be considered less likely to have to work all day to support a family, took their compulsory turns as watchmen, patrolling their community all night long.

Like the constables, these men were unpaid. Every able male had to serve his turn and the constable was the supervisor. The watchmen questioned travelers after dark, detained suspicious persons, and kept watch for criminal activities.

Actually, this seemingly casual kind of law enforcement worked. At least, it worked so long as it was limited to small compact groups where the force of public opinion could be swiftly rallied against an offender, and against any laxity or evasion of responsibility by any member of the group. For some six hundred years after the Statute of Winchester, English law enforcement rested almost solely on the concept of each individual's personal responsibility for his group.

Hue and Cry

One of the methods of mustering community support was *hue and cry,* which was a general alarm raised in the country upon any felony being committed. When *hue and cry* was raised, every person, by command of the constable, had to pursue the felon on pain of fine and punishment. The practice was in use at least as far back as Edward I (1239-1307), and in the society of the time, simplified the discovery and capture of persons fleeing from justice. It was used as late as 1735, since a statute of George II's was enacted that year decreeing that a constable who neglected to make *hue and cry* was to be fined five pounds (about twenty-five dollars at that time).

In essence, *hue and cry* was a kind of arrest.

The Watch

In the 1500's the men who kept order in the streets became known simply as "the Watch."

In Old Testament times the Hebrews divided the night into three watches, or periods of time, during which guards or sentinels were on duty to protect certain places, and the people and things in those places. The periods were from sunset to 10 P.M.; 10 P.M. to 2 A.M.; and 2 A.M. to sunrise.

The Romans increased the night segments to four: sunset to 9 P.M. (evening watch); 9 P.M. to midnight (midnight watch); midnight to 3 A.M. (cockcrow); and 3 A.M. to sunrise (morning watch).

To this day "watch" is a common term on land and sea to denote a specific period of time.

The people of Shakespeare's day knew the Watch* well, and the meaning of the name—those who watch, guard, protect—appears over and over in the literature of that day and has endured to the present.

However, the growth of communities made it finally very evident that law enforcement could no longer be safely based on the faith—no matter how lively—that the vast majority of citizens were law-abiding. In fact, with the passage of time this system of law enforcement began to break down. With community growth there came too many distractions and pressures for people to have any interest in being unpaid policemen in addition to their other obligations.

The inevitable happened: those who could afford to do so hired someone else to take their turn at watch. The quality of the substitutes dropped lower and lower until it became necessary for Charles II, after he was brought back from exile and restored to the English throne in 1660 (beginning the period, which lasted to 1688, known as the English Restoration), to provide a force of 1000 night watchmen, called bellmen.

Charlie, the Bellman

These bellmen, or watchmen, were the London police officers of the period. They were immediately dubbed "Charlies," a nick-

---

*For examples, William Shakespeare (1564-1616), in *Richard III* (Act 5, scene 3, line 54), has Richard say: "Good Norfolk, hie thee to thy charge; use careful watch, choose trusty sentinels."

In *Othello* (Act 2, scene 3, line 12) Cassio says: "Welcome, Iago; we must to the Watch."

In *Antony and Cleopatra* (Act 4, scene 3, line 18 a soldier says: "Let's see if other watchmen do hear what we do."

In *1 Henry IV* (Act 2, scene 4, line 536): "The Sherife and all the Watch are at the door: they are come to search the house. Shall I let them in?"

name as inevitable as the nicknames "Bobbies" and "Peelers" later given the paid policemen enrolled in London by Robert Peel.

Instantly the Charlies became the target of every cutthroat and tosspot in London, and it is a wonder that they survived. It has been a popular practice to downgrade the Charlies and to recount by rote their faults and shortcomings and failures. Faults they had, and serious ones, and shortcomings and failures, too. But if they were not always everything good lawmen should be, the blame was not entirely theirs. Their duties were discharged under conditions of persistent and unrelenting opposition and abuse which only the most dedicated could surmount.

Nobody demonstrated to get "rights" for the Charlies. They *had* no rights! All they had were responsibilities and obligations and duties, and they faced them and discharged them as well as they could. No matter how poor their performance, plagued as they were by unending harassment and intolerable working conditions, they still stood head and shoulders above the scum of the city, including some highborn scum of advantaged background, that they held in precarious check each night.

Among the Charlies were a substantial number of horrible examples, to be sure. There were the purchasable watchmen who could be bribed; there were the shirkers and connivers who, for a fee, could be depended on to be away from the scene of a planned criminal act; there were the blackmailers, who would give evidence for either side of a case.

But let us remember with equal clarity the good ones who night after night patrolled the filthy, reeking, unlighted streets with a courage it is hard to overpraise. Their only weapon was a staff which was sometimes too much for their strength to manage, weakened as they often were by age or hunger or weariness. Their clacker served chiefly to warn thieves of their approach or to pinpoint their location for the local rowdies to hunt down and torment. All but defenseless and forbidden to take action outside the strictly defined limits of their assigned areas, these men served their communities for a bare subsistence—without honor, without recognition, without much respect. Not one of them had any hope of reward for meritorious performance, yet nightly the best ones scorned many temptations to dishonesty or slack performance from thieves, fences, and house-breakers who asked only that the watchman turn his head for a moment.

In England until 1829 the watchmen were untrained citizens engaged in the complex and demanding task of guarding and protecting the life and property of others. As the police officers of those days, they stood all alone between the average citizen and chaos. Each was a lawman by instinct. Each possessed the traits of character which inclined him sooner to help than to hurt, sooner to build than to destroy, sooner to protect than to victimize, sooner to support and uphold the law than to attack and violate it. They asked no favors and sought no honor except the dignity of work and they worked, many of them, until they died on their rounds. Often enough they died alone, in some stinking alley, the sport of a pack of mindless bullyboys out on a lark.

Throughout history some baleful fortune has kept the watchmen chronically undervalued, underpaid, and undertrained. They have been subject to continual and merciless economic stress, and a population shift could make their job too big to handle or too small to require their service.

In London the population explosion made their job too big to handle and in the closing days of the century their reputation went from bad to worse. Fragmented, poorly supervised, lacking any central control, restricted in jurisdiction and action, and regulated by some 140 local and often contradictory Acts of Parliament, morale dropped to the vanishing point. More and more often the watchmen became accessories in aiding, abetting, or concealing the commission of crimes which it was their duty to detect and suppress.

When any community becomes so large that public opinion has no effect; when the threat of a unified action becomes empty; when laziness and indifference breed among the citizens; then the group has become far too large to have the unity necessary to control rowdyism and outrage. And at such a point, when self-policing is a wretched shambles and the thug and the hooligan learn they need fear no punishment, there is only one remedy that has ever worked: the community must obtain the help and the know-how of paid law enforcement personnel (whatever their title may be) under a competent chief officer, and this body of professionals must have no job but law enforcement.

The Watchman in the New World

In the New World we were doing no better. Despite the procession of historic events which changed us from a nation of hunters and farmers into a nation of scientists and manufacturers, our efforts at law enforcement did not—and do not today—keep pace with the increasing complexity of our lives.

During the 150 years Americans were under British rule—though thousands of miles removed from England—they were completely unable to support a body of paid police officers and equally incapable of training such a group if one existed. Furthermore, the fear and distrust of any paid and armed force was as rampant in the colonies as it was in the homeland. Accordingly, trapped between an ocean and a wilderness, the colonists learned quite a lot about taking care of themselves. The cornerstone of their protection was the simple law enforcement concept which said that the maintenance of law and order was the individual responsibility of each person, and that every citizen was accountable not only for his own actions but for those of his neighbors as well.

Such an ingrained sense of personal liability explains much of the "nosiness" of smalltown neighbors which for generations was the bane (and at the same time the protection) of towns and villages in this country.

The offices and duties of the English constable and sheriff were transferred almost unchanged to colonial America. The constable was responsible for law enforcement in the towns; the sheriff was responsible for law enforcement in the counties. Both were usually chosen by the government from among landowners loyal to the king. We had our tithingmen, who were hardly more than Sunday security officers, stationed at the meeting house to keep the children in (and under control), the dogs out, and the congregation awake through the service.

And the watchmen? Watchmen have appeared wherever and

whenever a local government was formed. Now they—with rattle and bell and hook and lantern and hourglass—were the police officers of a new nation, taking the side of the law-abiding inhabitants against those who would admit of no law except their own whims. At this point in history the colonial villages were huddled collections of ramshackle huts and covered cellars. Records, where any were kept, are today mostly in manuscript form, and details of the watchmen's performance exist chiefly in histories of the individual cities and towns and villages where watchmen were employed.

There was a citizens' watch in New York when the city was a place called New Amsterdam. In Boston in 1636 a town nightwatch was established which endured for 250 years through a variety of titles and mutations. Nearly two hundred years passed before the Boston watchmen were supported by a force of day police.

By 1700 the watchman was a familiar figure in American cities and towns, and for a full century thereafter he was a fixture in the exploding urban communities.

There were watchmen patrolling the streets of St. Louis from its founding in 1764 to the establishment in 1808 of its first police patrol—four men appointed to serve four months without pay. The patrol was staffed through a local requirement that all male inhabitants eighteen years of age and over, with a few exceptions, serve four months as a protector of the peace or provide a substitute.

Nowhere in letter or chronicle or report or book is there any indication that the watchman in this new land was one whit better off than he was in his original homeland. Here, as there, the work was unpaid, unhonored, and unappreciated. When the taxpayers' fear of an Indian attack or a slave uprising was acute, watchmen were hired and paid fifty cents a night. A night's work began about nine or ten o'clock in the evening, when the city gates were closed, and lasted until sunrise. When fears abated and the citizens would no longer tolerate even the tiny tax imposed for the watchmen's services, the mandatory duty to watch was imposed on each citizen in turn, usually on a day's notice. They were drafted just as soldiers were drafted for war service. Commonly excluded from service were boys, servants, magistrates, doctors, schoolmasters, shipmasters, paupers, clergymen, and those too ill or infirm to participate. Those excused were expected to keep the customary arms and ammunition in their homes.

The problems faced by watchmen in those times were not small. Fire was a calamity to be guarded against vigilantly; Indian attacks at night were an ever-present menace; hoodlums had to be prevented from tormenting friendly Indians; cholera epidemics flared too often and watchmen had to disinfect suspected sources of the disease; marauding animals and marauding humans—wolves, bears, wild dogs, thieves, cutthroats, grave-robbers—were nightly dangers to be faced and suppressed. Runaway slaves were a constant problem, and not only black slaves. There were white slaves, too. Some had been banished from England for their various crimes, as the laws of that country then permitted, and sold to pay their passage to this country; others—men, women, children—had been brazenly kidnapped and shipped to the colonies as laborers.

Watchmen were obliged to see that all disturbances were quelled, and to question all who walked abroad after curfew, which was commonly fixed at 10 P.M. in summer and 9 P.M. in winter. They were to arrest all who were drunk in public and all disorderly persons and disturbers of the peace. In some localities they regularly called out the time of night according to the town clock, and the kind of weather. In other places, however, they were instructed to go about quietly, using their bell or rattle only to summon aid. In places where street lighting existed, they usually were responsible for nightly trimming, filling, lighting, and extinguishing street lamps.

Watchmen worked only at night. Their patrol ended at sunrise, and they spent the days at other employment by which they supported their families. During the daytime there was no police protection of any kind for the citizens or their property. Many cities had two shifts of watchmen each night, each group—one-half of the Watch—working half the night, apparently on the theory that a watchman who worked all day could not reasonably be expected to work efficiently all night too. These watchmen were police officers and provided the only nighttime protection the community had, but when security is a secondary source of income—or a source of no income at all—it is apt to receive from a tired man less than his best efforts. Furthermore, the erratic alternating between paid volunteers and unpaid conscripts could not be, and was not, successful in controlling crime and violence in rapidly growing communities.

By the mid-1700's the watchman's job had become one to avoid, and all who could afford to do so hired others to serve in their place. More and more men defied the draft and preferred to pay a fine rather than serve. Constables were driven to select poor men to be watchmen. Poor men could be drafted and thus kept, with their families, off the relief rolls. They could be required to work without pay and receive, instead of money, credit on their tax debts. This is no way for a police organization to operate.

The Impossible Task

Colonization brought many races to these shores, and the races brought with them many an ancient grudge. From the beginning the Colonies were torn by wars and jealousies within and without. For more than a century before the Revolutionary War, intercolonial and Indian wars honed a bitter edge on provincial tempers. The dislocations of the ensuing peace strained to the snapping point the simple concept of self-policing which had survived intact an ocean crossing.

Counties turned their farmlands into industrial areas and seaports and transportation centers. Merchants and tradesmen began to outnumber the hunters and farmers. Villages grew into boisterous towns, and towns grew into unruly cities. The cities spread and attracted great numbers of people, and laws were passed to govern the people. Other laws were passed governing wages and labor contracts and street lighting and working conditions, and countless other areas of human endeavor.

The problems of protection grew steadily more complex. No longer, in the urban sprawl, did the concept of community responsibility for good behavior work. The watchmen tried. Nobody can say otherwise. As a class they were highly respectable, faithful, and dependable (with the usual, expected, and inevitable exceptions) and their failures were due more to lack of professional training and legal support than to any defect within themselves. Many of them, good family men and devout church members, had no business being watchmen. They did not like the work, had no taste for it, took no pride in it, showed no aptitude for it, developed no skill in it, and felt nothing but revulsion toward the dregs of the city they met night after night. They were not uniformed, they were not armed, they were not trained, they were not well supervised, and they were not adequately supported either by the magistrates or the jerry-built structure of local laws. There was no sound organization behind them, and there was no fraternal loyalty among them. In any locality the total number hired was increased or decreased almost on whim, and with no apparent rhyme or reason. Yet if incidents occurred which they could not or did not suppress promptly, the entire Watch was vilified and downgraded by people who had never in their lives worked for as little as fifty cents a night. It is not surprising that so many men preferred to be fined rather than to take a turn at this hard and lonely task.

In the 1800's sporadic attempts were made to strengthen the watchmen's position. Here and there, under above-average leadership their discipline toughened, their stations and rounds were fixed and supervised, neglect of duty brought punishment or dismissal, and whether on patrol or fixed post they were required to move immediately on command to any place where their assistance was required. While watchmen could not be firemen, they were regularly stationed at churches in order to have access to a loud bell in case of fire. They began to receive a small payment for court time resulting from action taken as watchmen.

The individual watchman's identification was a badge of leather buckled around a leather hat shaped something like a fireman's helmet. The badge carried the word POLICE and sometimes a number. Because of the hat he was called "Old Leatherhead," or, as an echo out of his past, "Old Charlie." He was still an untrained citizen, a part-time policeman, a tired man who worked all day in a tannery and did not have much stomach for wrestling hooligans in the streets at night. And he was still being regularly murdered on duty.

The end could have been foretold. Once again history repeated and the watchmen found the criminal odds against them hopeless, the mounting disorder impossible to contain.

There is no point in trying to assess or distribute blame. It is futile to hunt for a villain or a scapegoat; there is none. The country just grew too fast, and there was no form of policing at hand capable of managing this complex explosion of energy, of population, and of the democratic ideal which in effect said that whatever most people appear to want must therefore be right and good and just and fair and desirable.

What most people wanted, it sometimes seemed to the lawmen, was riots, gang fights, and mob terrorism. Such outbreaks were a plague in American cities which, in deep trouble, still temporized, still shunned the obvious solution, still rejected the idea of a professionally organized and trained force of law officers despite the successful example of London's metropolitan police. Instead they began to experiment with the addition of daytime "police" forces to support and supplement, but remain independent of, the night watchmen. Most cities of any size at the time tried this device, and in many cases long years passed before they began to challenge the ridiculous, costly, and inefficient spectacle of two official police forces in one city: one for the daytime and one for the night.

With recognition of the unwieldy and expensive condition the cities moved, one by one, to remedy the situation. In 1844 the New York legislature created law enabling formation of a single day-and-night police force, absorbing many watchmen into its ranks but eliminating watchmen entirely as a law enforcement entity. In 1846 St. Louis created a special department embracing the city marshal, the city guards, and the day police. Chicago followed and so, in due course, did most other cities that had tried the two-department experiment.

Sometimes the move was dramatic. Boston, for example, did

it literally in a matter of hours. One day in 1854 the mayor, with the support of the aldermen, fired every man on the watchmen's and policemen's rosters. Then from the combined lists he appointed the membership of a new Boston Police Department. It operated under a chief of police; every officer devoted his entire time to law enforcement and was permitted no other employment.

Sometimes, as in Chicago, the consolidation appeared as no more than a variation on existing procedure. A year after Boston's move Chicago created a police department and put a day patrol on regular duty without any abrupt or obvious change in duties or titles. The watchmen had been the police in Chicago and, years after the changeover, officers were still wearing the leather badge around their hats, carrying a club for a weapon and a rattle to call for assistance.

Eclipse

At about this time (roughly the beginning of the Civil War) the paths of the watchmen and the police, as we today understand the two titles, merged into a sort of blurred unity. Uniformed watchmen, or patrolmen, privately hired and paid, were "rented" to American businesses and industries. Titles became intertwined. Guards became police as we understand the term today. Police became detectives as we understand the term today. The watchman, meaning a peace officer with police powers, went into eclipse. There are now only local records and isolated monographs to tell us of their activities and services, and such records are far from complete. Books refer to manuscripts which no longer exist, and irreplaceable chronicles have vanished over the years, wiping out forever the information they contained. But still, traces can be found.

The explosive postwar expansion drove the boundaries of the new nation west and south and north to the border of Canada. The dregs of a dozen races made up the cutting edge of the immigrant wedge driving into the wilderness. These people when they were not causing trouble in their own vicinity, were making trouble among the Indians: smuggling rifles, smuggling alcohol, stealing horses, playing politics, and setting tribe against tribe.

And in the decades of the 1700's and 1800's, as the pioneers drove the frontiers of America to and beyond the Mississippi, to and beyond the Rockies, the watchman was, often enough, an Indian.

In the beginning, and before official authorization of an Indian Police Force in the late nineteenth century, almost any mounted and armed Indian, working under the instructions and authority of the local Indian agent, was a policeman. The title has always been as elastic as rubber, anyway. The Indians, enforcing white man's law on the reservation, also worked as guards for local coal companies, railroads, and mines. They protected stock for cattlemen, timber stands for logging companies, and fence lines for ranchers.

The decline of the Indian lawmen set in with the beginning of the twentieth century, at just about the time a contingent of uniformed private guards was policing the grounds of the Louisiana Purchase Exposition at St. Louis in 1904. A year later there were uniformed private guards on duty at the Lewis and Clark Exposition in Portland, Oregon. But pay remained low, efforts to attract superior personnel into private security were nonexistent, and business and industry made watchmen out of employees who were not temperamentally fitted for the job. Anybody who wanted to pick up a few dollars for sleeping on the premises and theoretically watching for fire could do so. A man who obtained a watchman's permit or commission had it forever.

Prior to and during World War I there was a great amount of sabotage, especially explosions and fires, attributed to enemy agents. In July 1916 saboteurs destroyed a munitions factory at Black Tom Island, a part of Jersey City. In 1917 a French munitions ship exploded in the harbor at Halifax, Nova Scotia (an important shipping center for the Allies), wrecking a large part of the city and killing more than two thousand persons. These and similar occurrences jarred some businessmen into an awareness of their extreme vulnerability and need for security assistance. For the most part, however, very little security consciousness was generated, and after the war industrial security departments returned to their original status as havens to which deserving employees could be retired as timekeepers, messengers, custodians, and watchmen—different titles, often enough, for the same set of duties.

Between the two World Wars, despite prohibition, crime waves, and industrial expansion, watchmen dropped into eclipse. When all is well, who needs them? And when the world comes apart and economic recession blots out the sun, who has anything to secure?

Except in a few instances, when premises security was not farmed out to one of the contract services, it became a marginal task loosely attended by custodial employees who, as often as not, shirked or ignored the responsibility. Where it was taken seriously, it seemed to cause as much grief as good. The industrial strife which was one of the ugly manifestations of the national agony known as The Great Depression of the 1930's tormented with a special viciousness the security men who were hired to protect shops and plants. They were often used by management as a weapon against other workers.

It was really not until the late 1930's, as the shadow of Armageddon darkened the earth, that industry went seriously into premises security. Most doubts and delays ended, at least temporarily, on December 7, 1941.

Early in World War I soldiers had been used extensively as guards around factories, utilities, and plants, but such use for the protection of private industry violated a principle credited to the then-Secretary of War, Newton D. Baker, that the plant itself and the local authorities were primarily responsible for industrial protection and plant security. So, with the outbreak of World War II, the privately licensed security officer leaped into the limelight, propelled by wartime pressures, needs, and problems. The problems included the huge numbers of men in military camps, the mass movements of people across the face of the country, the great industrial migrations to big cities and manufacturing centers, the social upheavals, and the dislocations of home life.

In a short time thousands and thousands of security officers— good, bad, and indifferent—were employed in premises protection. Communities that had never seen a security officer before began to use many of them. Usually the local police departments were responsible for their training. The old-time watchman began to fall into disrepute, and the awarding of the first flood of government defense contracts to manufacturers throughout the country sealed his fate. Sabotage and espionage were ever-present threats, and the need for better property protection became not only obvious but urgent. The government, apparently not impressed by the generally sorry state of national security, decided to bring plant watchmen into the Army as an auxiliary to the military police. Under government prodding, the force of auxiliary military police expanded into the thousands, the tens of thousands, and the hundreds of thousands, ultimately becoming what may long stand as the largest industrial police force in history.

Before the end of the war more than two hundred thousand men were sworn in by the Internal Security Division of the War Department and signed an agreement which brought them under the Articles of War. Their primary duties were to protect war goods, products, supplies, equipment, and personnel at some ten thousand industrial plants and factories. Technically, they were in the Army, but they went home every night like other civilians, worked regular hours like other civilians, paid taxes like other civilians, and were hired and trained and outfitted by the owners and managers of the plants and factories holding government contracts. Their status as auxiliary military police did not accord them any preferential treatment nor any blanket deferment from draft classification or induction into the Army. So, once again, watchmen became policemen. They became military policemen this time, forming protective lines around the plants, the mines, the laboratories, the factories, the shipyards, and the transportation facilities of a nation desperately fighting a second World War.

Very few of the men who entered private security by way of the auxiliary program possessed any previous police experience. The War Department furnished officers to conduct training classes, but the class material was chiefly military courtesy, tactics, drills, and procedures. It was the local police department that usually provided the nuts-and-bolts fundamentals of law enforcement training. And the training officers found what they usually find: a lot of their students had the makings of excellent law enforcement officers. Apt, quick, interested, and eminently teachable, they became the vanguard of the new breed of security officers who would from that time on nudge and jostle and harry and replace the watchman types whose performance was not measuring up.

They learned subjects watchmen had never before been required to know: what constitutes a crime, the importance of evidence, patrol procedures, report writing, preservation of the peace, protection of life and property, imposition and support of blackout regulations, prevention of unauthorized entry, care and use of firearms, apprehension of criminals, and so on. This group of men was substantially reduced during the early part of 1944, because of the need for additional manpower by the Armed Forces.

Resurgence

As a result of experience in World War II many individual manufacturers recognized the value of maintaining a well-trained, well-disciplined security force. In a parallel development local chiefs of police (as well as the training officers who had been so gratified at the way their charges responded to instruction) became interested in having manufacturers help solve growing security problems.

America's industrial expansion, fueled by two devastating wars in thirty years, left agriculture far behind, and the merchant and the tradesman became the folk heroes. Big cities became bigger, and laws were enacted covering every aspect of life: wages, hours, employer-employee relationships, working conditions, wealth, poverty, education, whatever you like. New operating techniques, processes, products, and properties brought legal controls with them, and the legal controls instantly brought exceptions and contradictory interpretations.

The problems of the police were staggering. The problems of the watchmen—usually none too well educated—became overwhelming and the security officer, quickly recognized as a different breed, began to be seen here and there. A knowledgeable man, with a liking for law enforcement and a knack for getting along with people, he got a job in private security wherever he showed up and asked. And he left as quickly as he could!

Why?

Because he had no difficulty in obtaining a better job with an insurance company as an investigator, with a trucking company as a transit officer, with a protection agency as a teacher and administrator.

And so America, facing into the end of the twentieth century bigger and more prosperous and possibly in greater danger than ever before, saw its best security officers seeking other employment because law enforcement did not pay a living wage.

II

THE PRESENT

Chapter Two

Private Security: A Modern Career

The Frightened Cities

I**T IS NOT DIFFICULT** to verify that we are living precariously in an age of lawlessness. The daily newspapers tell the story in every edition:

FEARFUL CITIZENS ARM AS CRIME RATE SOARS

CHURCH, PARISHIONERS UNITE TO EMPLOY GUARD

POLICE STATION FIRE BOMBED

TEEN-AGE HOODS TERRORIZE COMMUNITY

VIOLENCE AND FEAR CANCEL EDUCATION CONFERENCE

GUARD HIRED FOR INFORMATION CENTER

These headlines, collected at random over a weekend, are typical of thousands and thousands of similar stories that mirror our ugly national predicament.

Some say the causes of today's brazen lawlessness are complex and not well understood; some say the causes are understood but are so interlocked as to defy separation and successful treatment; some say the factors which encourage violence and the apparent trend toward anarchy include (1) laws disproportionately concerned with the rights of hoodlums and criminals and displaying little concern for the rights of law-abiding citizens and society in general. (2) prosecutors who fail to prosecute, and judges whose routine assessment of probation or light sentences have all but eliminated the criminal's fear of punishment; (3) the long period of time between arrest and trial, wherein witnesses can die or be intimidated while felons rove at liberty committing further crimes; (4) derelict courts and magistrates out of touch with reality; (5) the criminal's well-founded expectation of a light or suspended sentence and/or early parole; (6) the growing acceptance of the principle "if you don't like a law, don't wait to change it legally—violate it"; (7) the increasing amounts of time that must be spent by police officers in preparation of each individual case because of restrictions which practically require him to try his case when he seeks a warrant; and (8) citizens' distrust of police because of an occasional black sheep in uniform, and because of the loud, carefully staged hoodlum wailing about brutality which police, through cynical contempt or stubborn pride, do not trouble to combat or disprove.

Whatever the causes, the results are observable each day, and there is probably no longer anywhere a person or a piece of property which may be considered safe from criminal attack, vandalism, injury, theft, or destruction. Today, in any contest between the criminals and the law-abiding element, for control of a community, the criminals usually win.

In today's free society there sometimes seems to be only one free person: the criminal. Wholly free of any moral, ethical, or legal restraints, free of any fear or likelihood of control or discipline, he prowls the community almost at will, keeping the remainder of the population pretty well penned in. On such rare occasions when he is punished, it is by his own kind, not by the law-abiding members of the community. Any law-abiding citizen who shot a burglar breaking into his home would be immediately arrested for discharging a firearm within the city limits or for flourishing a dangerous and deadly weapon or (who knows, in this upside-down day?) for murder. In large city or small community the story is sickeningly the same.

Stores are beset by thieves from inside and from outside. Men are robbed and women have their purses snatched in broad daylight as they wait on the corner for a bus. In office buildings records are vandalized, equipment sabotaged, and employees intimidated. In the corridors of grade schools intruders harass children and rob them of their lunch money. In high schools teachers are attacked and sometimes killed; students beat and shoot each other. In colleges and universities foul-mouthed bullies disrupt classes, neutralize the administration, and burn buildings without fear of punishment or reprisal. Banks keep their money in their vaults and the amount at each teller's position must be "reasonable" according to the elastic wording of the Federal Bank Protection Act. Bus drivers do not carry change, gas stations do not keep change—the customer must come up with the exact amount for fare or for gasoline, or walk. Hospitals, museums, and government buildings are equally targets for thieves and vandals: food and linens disappear from hospitals; museums and zoos have valuable specimens wantonly maimed, damaged, killed; cash and stamps vanish from post offices; marinas have lights, buoys, and navigational guides wrecked or stolen. Innocent passengers on mass transportation vehicles are robbed and beaten and shot in broad daylight by teen-age hooligans who cannot be imprisoned because it might injure their personalities. In some cases their victims are dead and *they* walk free, without ever having been brought to trial. The riffraff, the deranged, and the vicious are taking over the streets, and their ranks are swelled each week by felons set free as quickly as courts and parole boards can defend release.

The Day We Live in

As a result we are living in a day when the public demand for security is insistent and nearly obsessive, a day when security and protection agencies are multiplying like the taxes promoted to "fight crime," when homeowners keep a loaded gun on each floor of their home, when guards and watchmen are hired sight unseen by people who have always been proud of their ability to take care of themselves.

We are living in a day when department stores open security corners where they display for sale all sorts of warning and protective devices for the person and the home. It is a day when security devices advertised in the columns of the daily newspaper include floodlights, fences, dogs, locks, chains, window bars, screens, firearms, tear-gas atomizers, wide-angle mirrors, one-way mirrors, sirens, closed circuit television, and alarms—space, fire, dial, intrusion, burglar, perimeter, silent, and automatic!

It is a day when feminine purses hold tear-gas cylinders along with lipstick and perfume; it is a day when the residents of any community will vote for any bond issue that is submitted as a crime-control measure; it is a day when police departments offer lessons in self-defense to women and in gun handling to businessmen.

It is a day when criminals roam free and keep the law-abiding in prison: locked in their homes, locked in their cars, locked in their places of business.

Churches, threatened with harassment and sacrilege, hold afternoon services and their perimeters are patrolled at night by security officers. Public libraries close earlier and theaters note an increase in ticket sales for afternoons. Merchants' associations unite to hire their own security patrols. In the evenings parks are unused, concerts go unattended, and citizens travel miles out of their way—on foot or by car, it makes no difference—to avoid the "core" areas of their cities.

People live with fear. They install alarms in, on, around their homes and businesses. Instead of gauze screens, they put steel bars on their windows. They fence their property about and turn sentinel dogs loose to roam the premises at night.

No longer do they stroll in their neighborhoods of an evening. Instead, they take instructions in self-defense at a gym class in the afternoon. For a pet they keep an attack dog instead of a cat or a sweet-tempered pup. Homeowners who never in their lives locked a door now bolt and bar their homes and look first through a peephole when a knock comes.

Men and women who never owned a gun, nor fired one, are now buying them. Housewives in isolated areas carry shotguns when they go outside to hang the family wash.

Many of these people, gently reared, openly express a willingness to point such a weapon at another human being and pull the trigger, on the cold estimate that creatures capable of the violent and heartless acts daily reported are not human at all and do not merit consideration as such. Whether these people could perform as unemotionally as they talk is an open question, with the answer dependent on many circumstances. It is not a question important in this chapter. What *is* important is the way people are changing. The reasons why they are changing are important too. They are changing for the same reasons that they are coming to rely on bolts and bars and guns rather than on laws and attorneys and courts of justice. They are changing because they suspect that the total number of *un*reported crimes is conservatively equal to, and probably greater than, the number of reported crimes.

They are changing because for so many weary years they have watched the depressing parade of inept prosecutors, ineffectual judges, and bleeding-heart juries obsessed with the rights *(never the responsibilities)* of the criminals who have openly declared war on society, that they no longer believe there is in this country an agency of government that cares a fig about the victims of crime.

They are changing because they are coming to believe that reporting a crime, or depending on the courts for justice, is a waste of time.

This Is a Showup

Have you ever attended a showup at a police station? There, on the brightly lighted stage behind the dusty black mesh curtain, slouch the scum of the city, netted in the previous night's patrol. Moments ago they came shuffling from the holdover, slovenly in appearance and manner, bitter with rage at having been caught. There is here no shame or regret or remorse for the injury they have done their victims—only a snarl for the officer reading the charge and a blind sullen stare for the witnesses watching from the black pit outside the lighted stage.

Look at the greasy group standing against the black wall with the horizontal white lines indicating their height. Listen to the roll call of animals who lurk in ratty basements or prowl the streets in packs to mug or snatch purses from people unable to fight back, to cripple or kill for ninety cents, to steal and rob for kicks:

"Donald Wayne Genske, giving an address of 3640 Virginia, arrested by Officer Boyland of the Third Precinct and held on a charge of burglary, warrant issued. Also held for authorities in Huntsville, Alabama, for issuance of bogus checks. Donald Wayne Genske. Stand where you were please. . .

"Arrested at 2151 Wheaton by Detective Farmer of the Bureau of Investigation, Hobart Wesley Bolden, giving an address of 1800 Theodosia. This man is held on charges of armed robbery, two counts, two warrants issued. Hobart Wesley Bolden. Stand back where you were. . .

"Marvin Bell, giving an address of 472 Wellington, held for violation of the state narcotics laws, arrested by Officer Day of Narcotics Bureau. Stand back in line, please...

"As your name is called, take two steps forward...

"Joseph Walcz, giving an address of 1331 Washington, arrested by Officer Mullins of Central District. This man is held for criminal assault and carrying a concealed weapon, two warrants issued. Also charged with fraudulant use of a credit device, warrant also issued. Prior record indicated. Joseph Walcz."

If you were a security officer, any one of these men could last night have been prowling the property you were assigned to protect. Mere hours ago you might have cornered one of them and held him for police. Listen:

"Arrested at 3708 South Grand by Officer Miller of Third Precinct, Daniel Harvey Speedy. This man is held suspected of aiding and abetting vice, warrant issued. Prior record indicated. Daniel Harvey Speedy. Stand back where you were, please...

"Arrested 3104 Pier Street by Officer Whelan of Third Precinct, Lawrence Clarence Black, giving an address of 1492 Albert, held suspected of homicide. Prior record indicated. Lawrence Clarence Black, stand back where you were."

Make no mistake about these people. Their minds do not work like yours. Their minds do not work in any way you would consider rational. They laugh and they cry, but their laughter and their tears are not yours. They laugh to see pain and humiliation and grief; they cry only to avoid a rare threat of punishment.

"Arrested at 2135 Landsman by Officer Roche of Special Operations, Edward Daniel Thomas, giving an address of 2121 New England, held suspected of stealing over fifty dollars, an automobile, and assault with intent to do great bodily harm. A prior record is indicated. Edward Daniel Thomas, stand back where you were...

"Homer Ricardo Wesley, arrested at 2000 Dumont by Sergeant Foreman of the Bureau of Investigation. This man gives an

address of 5213 Kenosha. He is held for one count burglary, two counts armed robbery, three warrants issued. Homer Ricardo Wesley. Stand back, please...

"Also arrested at 2000 Dumont by Sergeant Foreman of the Bureau of Investigation, Herbert Perry, Jr., alias Alfred Terry, Jr., alias Terry Herbert, giving an address of 1438 Austin. This man is held for armed robbery, two counts, two warrants issued. Herbert Perry, Jr., alias Alfred Terry, Jr., alias Terry Herbert. Stand back where you were...

"Everybody stand up straight. Take off your hats. Drop your hands to your sides. Look straight out to the front. Right face. Go through that door to the right at the far end."

The lights on the stage go out and the lights in the showup room go on. You come out of the jungle, back to the orderly world which is orderly only because there are police officers and security officers to keep it so.

The Police Manpower Squeeze

Keeping it so is not easy. The task of providing safety, security, and well-being for the persons and property of decent citizens—citizens for whom the crime rates are literally matters of life and death— is formidable.

Some years ago police officers won the just and proper right to a forty-hour work week. Every fair-minded citizen approved the humane revision of working hours, and few thereafter thought any more about the matter. Yet the effect the change had on the police manpower situation was profound.

To picture the resulting problems let us consider the city of Riversite, in the geographical middle of the United States.

Riversite covers an area of sixty square miles. It encompasses one thousand miles of improved streets, four hundred miles of alleys and unimproved streets, and twelve miles of riverfront.

According to the latest census, Riversite has a population of 750,000 citizens. Actually, at high noon of any day the population may easily be an even million persons because of the daily influx of transients, shoppers, visitors, and the suburban residents employed in Riversite's business, industry, and commerce.

The city has a police force of two thousand commissioned officers when it is at authorized strength, which is seldom.

The authorized strength works out to fewer than three officers for each one thousand inhabitants, and two officers for each one thousand inhabitants of the midday population when the city is most active. Both figures are close to the national average for all cities in the United States, though below the national average for cities of Riversite's size. The national average for cities of Riversite's size at this writing is slightly more than three officers for each one thousand citizens. This assumes, of course, that Riversite's force is always at full, authorized strength, and that all officers are available for duty. This ideal situation never happens. Resignations, retirements, and recruitment difficulties plague Riversite no less than other communities in the nation. There are four hundred Riversite officers—many of them limited-performance officers who have been injured in the line of duty—regularly engaged in specialized administrative, supervisory, and training duties at various precincts in the city, acting as court officers, or assigned to special details (parades, sports events, funeral or VIP escorts) and assignments (homicide, arson, burglary, vice) around the clock. Eight hundred more will not be available for duty because of illness, injury, vacation, compensatory time off for overtime already served, courtroom appearances, preparatory paperwork on cases, and the limitations of the forty-hour week.

In other words, at any specific hour of the day or night, Riversite has 60 per cent of its police automatically removed from crime fighting and preventive patrol. This leaves eight hundred men to do police work over twenty-four hours in a city with a daytime population of approximtely one million inhabitants. That equals 267 officers for each eight-hour watch (shift).

To put it another way, in the city of Riversite, where on any average day a million people work and play and test the laws of an ordered society, there will be on street patrol at any one time one officer for each 3,846 citizens. Or 4.45 officers per square mile, which is stretching the line of protection thin indeed.

Anyone who thinks that this number of men can contain all the problems and happenings which develop in a city of one million people, enforce fairly and with justice the countless laws and ordinances, and at the same time act as guide, mentor, friend, judge, jury, father confessor, crossing guard, city directory, and rescuer of treed cats has completely lost touch with reality.

Add the soaring number of citizen requests for police service —double in the past ten years and still climbing—and the unchanging total number of police officers (forty-five officers have been added to the Riversite force in the past ten years) and you begin to understand why the entire security officer concept is undergoing radical reevaluation among knowledgeable police administrators.

The Reinforcements

Riversite is luckier than many cities, although almost any city could be equally lucky given Riversite's initiative and foresight and smart police chief. It has about two thousand security officers, licensed by and responsible to a Security Division set up in the police department solely to instruct, control, and supervise them. These security men are employed by some three hundred businesses, industries, corporate entities, and trade associations in the city, by more than forty contract protection agencies and, in some two dozen instances, by themselves as self-employed beat officers. (The self-employed beat officers are private patrolmen who have contracted with clients in certain areas of Riversite to supply security services, and whose property they visit and inspect, for a set weekly fee, a certain number of times each night according to the individual instructions of each client. The self-employed beat officers are licensed and regulated by the Riversite police department just like other security officers.) Included among the licensed security officers in Riversite are more than one hundred retired police officers and nearly three hundred active police officers moonlighting in secondary employment.

Are these security officers of any help to the Riversite police officers? In a recent ten-month period surveyed by the Riversite department of police, this supplementary force of officers detained or arrested 171 suspicious persons—144 men and twenty-seven women; handled efficiently thirty-six burglaries, eighteen robberies of all types, seven larcenies, sixty-five stealing attempts, eleven credit card frauds, eighteen disturbances of all types, four passing of bogus checks, eleven cases of malicious destruction of property, eleven assault and carrying of a concealed weapon, five auto thefts and attempts, and 9 miscellaneous, including trespassing, resisting arrest, and vehicle tampering. In the discharge of their duties thirty-seven shots were fired by these officers; goods and money in the amount of $1,111.13 were recovered. And forever unknown, with no way in the world to find out, remains the number of crimes which were never attempted simply because these men and women were on the job. This is a good record. This is good law enforcement. Any person interested in being where the action is could do a lot worse than join these security officers.

The Watchmen

If and when you enter private security you are going to find there ahead of you men and women who will be, according to your standards, a pretty sorry lot. Indeed, you may have trouble recognizing them as belonging to the security profession if you have been fortunate enough to know only well-trained, well-supervised, modern security officers. They will be in the waiting room with you when you go to have your application processed—the loud, the ignorant, the sly, the slovenly, the faintly suspect,—and you will not willingly accept them as equals.

"Who," you will wonder, " *are* these people?"

They are watchmen, mostly. Or they will be watchmen when they become licensed. They are not now, nor will they ever be, security officers. They do not especially want to be security officers, nor do most of them realize that there is a difference between a watchman and a security officer. What far too many of them want is the quickest route to a gun permit.

Several times each month there can be seen on the desk of any licensing officer a pad of individually addressed letters awaiting the officer's signature. The letters are identical. Each is addressed to an applicant who has sought a license as a private security officer. Each rejects the application "on basis of our background investigation." What did the background investigations reveal? They revealed criminal records concealed and denied by applicants, they revealed dishonorable military discharges concealed and denied by applicants, they revealed felony convictions, mental instability, gross neglect of responsibility in previous employment, and unacceptable medical history—all concealed and denied by applicants on their written, signed, falsified applications.

If you ask the licensing officers why, after years of effort to upgrade security employment, so many applications are still being submitted by riffraff, he will review for you the well-known drawbacks of security work. Long hours, low pay, inadequate supervision—the whole list. Then he will get to the point: "Most of this disappointing condition can be blamed on a widespread and persistent belief which has endured for five hundred years—the belief that no matter how eccentric, incompetent, unlettered, undependable, and downright unteachable a person is, he can always scrounge a few dollars as a watchman."

In those words lies perhaps the heaviest burden of the modern security officer, who has not been able to live down—not even with his best efforts—the reputation for inefficiency and carelessness which for years has tended to tarnish the name of private security.

It is a tarnish which may not brighten soon, and a burden which may not lighten soon, because the passive watchman—the yardstick by which the modern security officer measures the distance he has traveled toward professional competence—is still with us in awesome numbers, fashioned by many forces.

Security agencies make watchmen. Sometimes it is difficult to escape the impression that the lax standards of the outdated watchman are being deliberately fostered by some agencies, judging by the caliber of the personnel they appear willing to hire and assign—to hire and assign, often enough, with the full knowledge that the individuals have already been rejected by the local licensing authority.

Individual employers make and perpetuate watchmen because they commonly do not know the difference between a watchman and a security officer. Worse, they often do not seem to care so long as the fee is not high, and if, after hiring a presence for their premises, employee theft remains serious or a fire burns beyond control or automobiles are looted on the parking lot, it is only to be expected since *all* security personnel are incompetent and *all* protection agencies are frauds. The money of such employers has been wasted, true enough, but the fault does not lie with private security.

Police officers and commanders make watchmen. They make watchmen by their attitude of "If you want to be a police officer join the department!" The police officer who says that, or implies it, appears neither to know nor to care that often the object of his scorn does want to be a policeman, and would make a good police officer. But the vocation came late and now the candidate cannot meet the age limitations; or he dropped out of school just a few scholastic credits short; or he found the vocation after he had hung up a checkered employment record and a jail sentence he bitterly regrets.

By dictionary definition a watchman is one who keeps watch or guard; one formerly assigned to guard the streets of a city by night; one who is employed to stand watch over, or to patrol, property to protect it against fire, theft, vandalism, or any loss or damage; one who, for pay, guards or protects people, places, and things.

Historically this has been the watchman's role, but it is more and more being taken over by security officers. Why? Because the security officer does a better job. In a few minutes you will be reading about security officers, and you may think to yourself: How is this definition of security officers and their work so much different from what I was reading about watchmen a few pages back? The difference lies in the attitude of the security officer toward law enforcement work, in the expanded scope of his responsibilities, in the standards of performance required of him, and in his bearing and demeanor on the job.

A watchman will usually exhibit lower standards of performance than a security officer. He will not have to meet any strict requirements for employment, his duties will be minimal and mechanical, and he may even be expected to do custodial chores during his hours of employment.

A watchman—as here defined—tends to be a bit lazy. Once on a job and without meaningful supervision he will see criminal activity and take no action because if he takes action it means writing a report and going to court and that is too much trouble for the money he is getting.

A watchman is inclined to discharge his duties in a cursory manner. Watch him perform one of his simplest jobs: watch him lower the flag at the end of the day. He will spin it down the pole, wad it into a ball, and throw it on some nearby bushes or onto the ground while he fixed the halyard. Then he picks up the flag, still rolled into the likeness of a bundle of soiled laundry, jams it under his arm, and takes it to the guard room where he tosses it into a corner to await the morning. Security officers raise and lower the flag with respect, fold it properly for storage, and carry it in a flat square to the guard room.

A watchman tends to slip downhill fast. First he stops shining his shoes, then he stops tying the laces; then, when he cannot find the black belt he should wear with his uniform, he wears a brown one to hold up his unpressed trousers. The shirt he wore yesterday looks good enough to wear again today, and in a very short period of time you have a "security officer" who would fit unnoticed into the lobby of a cage hotel.

Now, from this man withhold training, since training is expensive to provide; withhold incentive, which is the mainspring of any man's ambition; withhold supervision, which confirms his conviction that nobody cares much what he does, and you have a security problem instead of a solution.

Blame these people? No. Reclaim these people? Probably not. Why? Because we are talking about men who, at least until a very short time ago, are—or were—in an age bracket which rejects training. Worse, we are talking about men who have frequently been so exploited by their employers in the process of making all possible profit, that they no longer believe they have any personal worth of their own. They can be conscientious and loyal within their limits, but it is impossible to get written reports from them. Count it satisfactory if they sign their time sheets. They have acquired, in one way or another, a rigid concept of their job, of what the job requires of them, of what they must do and what they do not have to do, and if the concept does not mesh with good modern security practice, that is unfortunate because that is all they have to offer an employer.

Let us meet Frank Lee Dull, a good watchman, and see him as Police Lieutenant Larry Diehl saw him one evening in late September.

At dusk this cool autumn evening Lieutenant Diehl, the Watch Commander, was making a tour of his district. He halted his car at the foundry gate and waved to the nondescript man in the visored cap who was lounging against the turnstile.

Diehl did not recognize the man who, responding to his wave, straightened and moved slowly across the broad sidewalk to the window of the police car.

" 'Evening, Lieutenant."

The Lieutenant nodded.

"You the watchman? I don't remember seeing you here before."

"You're right, Lieutenant. I just came on tonight. Mike is off sick and the boss sent me down."

"Who's your boss?"

"Nightowl Security."

"You have a license?"

"Right here, Lieutenant."

"O. K.," the Lieutenant said pleasantly, "Stay awake and if you need any help, yell."

He put the car into gear and paused, regarding the watchman thoughtfully.

"You know the district number, right?"

"Don't worry, I can find it quick enough if I need it."

The number of working watchmen who have no idea of the police department telephone number they are supposed to use (or, for that matter the fire department number, the hospital number, or their employer's number) is appalling. These telephone numbers are basic equipment and they belong in a security man's head, not in the telephone book. They are his source of help in time of trouble. If he needs help, he needs it *now*, not after he has searched through a telephone directory.

Lieutenant Diehl, never taking his eye from Frank's face, nodded slowly. Then, almost hopelessly, he began to raise the car window.

Self-importantly the watchman drew back his jacket and thrust a shiny serge hip into the lieutenant's line of vision.

"See? I've got my own gun."

The Lieutenant flicked the gear shift back into neutral and lowered the car window.

"I'm a gun enthusiast," he said. "What kind is that? I don't remember the configuration."

"It's a revolver," said the watchman.

"I know, but what kind?"

"I don't know. A Russian kind, I think."

"You *think?* Don't you have a permit for it?"

"Yes I do. Right here," and he reached for his wallet.

"Never mind," said the lieutenant. "I'm sure you have a permit. But haven't you ever handled this piece?"

The watchman shook his head.

"I ain't never fired a gun in my life."

Now, let's suppose for a moment that this watchman—a good man, a sincere man, and a dangerously untrained man—had been backed into a corner in an incident which forced him to draw and use his weapon to protect his own life or the life of another. Who would be in danger? The person threatening him? Probably not. If an untrained shooter hits the thing at which he thinks he is aiming the first time he squeezes the trigger, it is an accident. Nobody draws and fires a revolver for the first tme and scores a bull's-eye except by accident. As a matter of fact, probably everyone in the vicinity, including the watchman, *except* the person at whom the watchman was shooting, would be in danger.

Here is an example of a man trying to perform a complicated task with no instruction, no support from his supervisors, and no real awareness of his perpetual danger. He should not have been engaged at all in the hard, often dangerous, job to which he had been assigned by an employer who was interested only in the fee to be obtained by furnishing a warm body at the foundry. No amount of training or supervision will make security officers out of such men. Watchmen stay watchmen. Good watchmen, perhaps, but watchmen nonetheless. The public practice of identifying as watchmen all lawmen who are not police officers is an enduring vexation to the security officers. So is the widespread community practice of issuing to such men a badge and a shoulder patch labeling them watchmen. The true security officer is *more* than a watchman, in temperament and in performance.

The Security Officers

It would be ridiculous indeed to pretend that all security officers are inspired by the ideals which form the core of this book. However, a sufficient number of them are so inspired as to be in themselves inspiring.

It was nearly three o'clock in the morning and as Security Officer Nick Raisor came down the inside fire stairs of the motel and pushed through the door into the lobby he shook his head irritably. He was tired and he was missing something. There was something he was not tuning in. And that vague uneasy thought was nearly his last on earth.

As the fire door clicked shut behind him, his glance angled off a dozen feet to his right where three men stood at the registration desk. Two held revolvers on the night clerk who was putting money into a large purse standing open on the desk. A third man, armed with a shotgun, stood a few feet away, partly hidden by a lobby pillar. It was this man who heard the fire door close, and he swung around, his shotgun leveled.

Raisor yelled: "Hold it. Police." He flung himself to the floor just as the shotgun went off. Three against one is television stuff, but Raisor played the cards he had. From the floor, his left arm a flaming, twisted agony from his fall, he got off three shots at the trio. They fled, leaving the purse and the money on the registration desk. Raisor followed the men. He reached the semicircular driveway in front of the motel just in time to see a darkened car whirl into the street and head north. The shotgun was lying in the driveway. As the car roared away, shots were fired from it at Raisor, who returned the fire and went pounding out to the street. There he halted, held his revolver against his body with his nearly useless left arm, and reloaded as fast as he could. Two blocks away, well within Raisor's view, the car stopped and the three men, and the woman who had been driving, fled on foot in different directions.

Meanwhile, the night clerk had called the police; the patrol car, coming from the north, arrived in time for the officers to see the abandoned car standing in the street with lights burning and all four doors open, the shadowy scattering figures and the security officer running toward them.

Raisor climbed into the patrol car with the two police officers and they began to scour the neighborhood. Raisor spotted one of the men—the one who had fired the shotgun—on the street a few blocks away and halted him. The holdup man offered no resistance and said only, "You've got me. I'm one of them." The prisoner, booked suspected of robbery and assault with intent to kill, showed no inclination to take all the blame. He was advised of his rights but could not wait to name his friends.

One newspaper, next day, ran the story under a headline that said WATCHMAN RISKS LIFE, ROUTS BANDITS. Another paper said GUARD HALTS ROBBERY AT MOTEL.

Raisor does not mind. He knows that newspapers have space problems and that "watchman" and "guard" contain fewer letters than "security officer." He knows that he is a watchman and that he is a guard. He also knows that he is a security officer.

A security officer is any person duly constituted under applicable laws and ordinances and possessing the duty and responsibility to guard and care for persons and/or property under the terms of an employment contract (actual or implied), and whose service includes, but is not necessarily limited to, insuring the adequate protection of the building, homes, and property—together with their contents and personnel—within the boundaries of his jurisdiction by a constant patrolling for the purpose of watching and guarding the area assigned to him for such protection.

". . . *whose service includes, but is not necessarily limited to . . .*"

Few people realize the variety of duties a modern security officer is expected, even required, to perform.

The basic, fundamental duties of watching, guarding, patrolling, and protecting have been substantially expanded and a security officer is expected to assist police officers in protecting life and property, keeping the peace, preventing crime wherever possible, anticipating it routinely, apprehending felons and holding them for the police.

He must decide in a moment whether a specific illegal act coming to his attention is a felony or a misdemeanor. Should he arrest the violator, or would it be wiser to let the incident pass with a warning? If he decides on an arrest, he must have the facts to support his decision because an arrest is meaningless lacking the intent to carry it straight on to a conviction, which requires testifying to *facts*. He must know the elements of legal arrest, the involved area of search and seizure, and the routines of the criminal courts. He is expected to be a man of courage, ready to respond immediately and successfully to any sudden emergency. He must solve problems he never experienced in his life and do so promptly and with a maximum of tactful diplomacy.

He must know what he is seeing when he looks at a con man, a pigeon drop, a cardsharp, or a mentally unbalanced troublemaker.

He is a teacher, alerting citizens to safety practices and procedures. He is a traffic control officer directing pedestrian and vehicular flow during changes of shift at industrial plants. He is Authority, keeping order at public functions, parades, indoor and outdoor sporting events, displays of valuables (furs, paintings, jewelry, guns, coin and stamp collections, and so on) .

It is expected that on any assignment he will immediately become acquainted with the property, neighborhood, and terrain to which he is assigned, normal procedures in his area, materials, supplies, equipment, furnishings, and personnel within the area of responsibility. Such familiarity is essential if he is to notice and identify variations which might spell trouble, variations which could be silent warnings of something not quite right, something that needs prompt investigation and a satisfactory explanation plus a report to the employer.

He will be alert for, and will promptly report to his employer or to the police, or both, all instances of questionable conduct occurring on his beat or in his jurisdiction before a serious stage of law violation has been reached. He also helps by reporting hazards to public safety (a burned-out street light, for example) and suspicious circumstances such as open doors or windows, and lights in vacant buildings.

Because of the very life he lives, he is often more knowledgeable than parents, friends, teachers, social agencies, or probation officers in spotting conditions and situations which should be reported to the police.

He makes an arrest when that is what he must do, tells the police why he did it, and turns his prisoner over to the police. It makes no difference to him that it is the police officer's name which goes on the record as making the arrest. Police departments know, and police officers know, how often it is a security officer's information which makes it possible to obtain a warrant, how often a culprit is detained by a security officer until the police arrive, how often it is the testimony of a security officer that clinches the conviction.

He has no say in the results of his efforts or his apprehension of the lawbreaker. Many times he sees culprits freed and his best efforts brought to nothing. Being human, when this happens he has human feelings of cynicism, frustration, indifference, and discouragement, and he is expected to suppress them and get back to work.

He is not a prosecutor. He is a peace officer upholding laws other men have made, and doing it as impartially as a human being can do it.

For example, Security Officer Pat Draug noticed the gross woman the moment she entered the diner. It would be impossible to overlook her. She was not tall, she weighed more than three hundred pounds, her lank, unwashed black hair hung about her sweating, stupid face. She had been drinking heavily.

Draug was assigned to the drive-in Blacktop Diner at the edge of town—a modest business with a transient and unpredictable clientele, a reputation for excellent take-home food, and an isolated location.

This Sunday night the take-out line was long. Draug, standing relaxed inside the diner entrance, compressed his lips, shook his head once as the coarse woman pushed in, and then let his eyes, ever on the move, rove over the interior looking for possible problems.

His attention was jerked back to the take-out counter and he tensed against the wall. The huge woman, ignoring the line of patient customers, had lumbered directly to the counter where she began screaming curses at the girls preparing orders to go.

Quickly Draug moved to the side of the woman and said quietly, "It will be necessary for you to take your place in line, Ma'am. We'll wait on you just as soon as we can but all these other people were here first."

The woman turned on Draug like a spitting cobra, her mouth open to spew vulgarity through snagged and blackened teeth. "I don't care a goddam who was here first. If you're the police just step outside and I'll blow your goddam head off."

"Nobody wants any trouble, Ma'am," Draug said patiently. "If you don't want to take your place in line, I'll have to ask you to leave. You're disturbing the customers."

"The hell with the customers," the huge woman screamed. "Don't put your filthy hands on me, you hear?"

Draug, who had reached out to take the woman's elbow, withdrew his hand. "Nobody wants any trouble, Ma'am," he repeated, "but you'd better leave. You're disturbing the customers."

"Nobody's putting me out," shrieked the woman. "I don't care if you are the police. You try to put me in jail and I'll shoot you."

At these words the woman thrust a hand into her shapeless dress, and Draug, fearing for his safety, dove forward. He flung his arms around the woman's massive shoulders, momentarily pinning her arms, and at the same time drove his lowered head into her throat. His hat flew off. The stench from her—sweat, booze, filth— all but suffocated him. As he held on grimly, the woman tried to shake free, stumbled and went down.

The crowd watched silently. One girl of the four behind the counter had enough sense to put in a call for the police.

Draug broke away from the woman and moved swiftly to the

door. He opened the door and, with a quick backward glance to make sure that the woman saw him, moved out to the parking lot. There, at least, he would have room to maneuver a little.

"Call the police," he called to the countergirls, and went out, pursued by the slobbering woman who kept screaming that nobody was going to put her in jail. Customers on the parking lot crowded around an open space to see the "fun." His back against the side of a truck, Draug faced the lumbering woman, coming at him like a tank, screaming unbelievable obscenities as she moved.

Draug unsnapped his tear-gas canister and held it in front of him, thumb on the button.

"You are under arrest for peace disturbance," he warned. "Don't make things worse for yourself . . . ."

And then, from a few blocks away, came the sweetest sound a man in trouble can hear: the siren of a police cruiser.

The sound seemed to penetrate the woman's mental haze and she stopped, and it was that way the police officers found them. In the center of a circle of expressionless watchers stood Draug, hatless and with a shirt torn at the shoulder, holding a tear-gas canister at the ready, aimed at a monstrous woman who stood planted like a sumo wrestler, swaying a little and staring at Draug with murder in her piggy eyes.

The officers, acting on Draug's information, arrested the subject on a charge of individual peace disturbance and advised her of her rights. She declined to make a statement, at which time one of the officers contacted the record room at police headquarters by radio and learned that there was a bench warrant out for the subject, charging failure to possess a state driver's license and driving while intoxicated. The subject was then put into the police cruiser and transported to city hospital to be examined for possible injuries sustained in the struggle with Draug. Draug was informed that no further action would be taken on the peace disturbance charge unless he appeared personally at the office of the City Counselor within five days.

Draug, his right hand at his left shoulder absentmindedly holding together the edges of his ripped shirt, nodded that he understood, and went back into the diner to look for his hat. His wife would just have to make the shirt wearable; he could not afford a new one right now, not until he got daughter Katy's dental bill paid.

How do we get such men! How do we keep such men! Thankfully there is a growing awareness of the value of our security officers and a growing ability to identify them.

Briefly, the real difference between a security officer and a watchman is this: When a security officer tenders five years of experience, he delivers five years of learning, studying, and broadening in the techniques and procedures of law enforcement; when a watchman tenders five years of experience, he delivers one year of experience repeated five times, or perhaps one day of experience repeated 1,825 times.

Let It End!

If you—a security officer candidate—listen, and do not care to whom you listen, you can hear all sorts of horror stories about the touchy relationships between security officers and police officers. On the other hand, investigation shows that most of the security officers who have trouble with police officers are the same dunces who always have had trouble with police officers.

It is a rare occasion when a security officer of tact, competence, or dignity has trouble with a police officer. Despite rumors to the contrary, police officers are not entirely witless. They like to have people on their side, and they do not go out of their way, ever, to make enemies. There is not a knowledgeable police officer in the world who is not glad to have a trained, trusted security officer as his friend on the street: a man prepared to *help* with law enforcement problems instead of *being* one of them.

Just so you know what police officers have bothering them, consider the following:

Citizen crime-control efforts are nothing new. As already mentioned, no paid police force existed in the United States before the early nineteenth century. If the sheriffs, constables, and watchmen could not enforce the laws, the militia was called in. Sometimes it could not reach the trouble spot for several days.

Today there is probably no city of consequence in the United

States that has not tried, or does not presently have, some form of citizen participation in law enforcement activities; but with monotonous regularity police departments have seen the citizens reserve, or the auxiliary police, or the security patrol, or whatever it is called, taken over by the disruptive elements of the community to enforce their own version of "freedom" and "law and order" and "crime control." Where that does not happen, the auxiliary invariably begins to push—under the guise of giving more help to the police—to be armed, and to get the power to arrest, and nine times out of ten it winds up not as a help to, but as one more problem for, the police.

If you do not believe it can be a problem, just think about the precarious position of a couple of police officers investigating a robbery complaint in a high-rise apartment building which is being patrolled by two different groups of high-minded, helpful, nervous, armed citizens who all happen to be tenants of the complex and do not like each other very much!

And there's where the unhappy rub occurs. Rightly fearing the development of vigilantism, some police have not yet come to see security officers as different from other citizens. There is no doubt at all that the police-officer-in-training ought to receive more instruction than he does about the role of the security officer in modern crime control. Rarely is the existence of the security officer (whom the rookie will meet the very first day he goes out on the street) even mentioned in training lectures. The result is that when the probationary patrolman goes out on his assignment, he is a bit uncertain about how to treat a privately licensed lawman who wants nothing more than to be a helpful friend. It is not the police officer's fault, and it is not the security officer's fault. It is just one of those regrettable gaps in communication which add up to a real loss for everyone.

Police officers do not like big headlines that say POLICEMAN JAILED across the top of a news story which relates how a former campus watchman was convicted of stealing from a student's unlocked room. And again, you will be disliked by some police who are overly conscious that today's smart, career-oriented police officer is a fairly recent evolutionary product. After all, it was not so long ago that it was assumed the police officer was a policeman because he could not be anything else. This is no longer, and was never entirely, true but all the same he sometimes tends to look on your very existence as a threat to his status and a reflection on the job he is doing. Your existence has nothing to do with him or with the kind of job he is doing and in his heart he knows this, but he still does not like you.

So try to be mature enough to realize that after spending years encouraging the idea that they are the experts in crime control and that they are the ones best equipped by ability, training, and experience to deal with crime and criminals, police officers do not find it easy to see the crime rate climbing apparently without hindrance. If your positions were reversed, might you not possibly tend to interpret an offer of assistance from private patrolmen as a cheap taunt, if not indeed as an outright expression of doubt about your competence?

Valid or not, these are reasons (and good reasons, if you are a police officer) why you may sometimes find the very men you unreservedly support looking at you with doubt and uncertainty. As long as these reasons are not substantiated by actions of yours, they have nothing in the world to do with you.

If you, a security officer, have trouble with a police officer, the odds are ten to one you will be the one that brings it on. If a police officer (or for that matter, if *anyone)* files a complaint against you it will be—in ninety-five instances out of every one hundred—because you have failed to act like, look like, and think like a professional security officer. You have talked too much, argued too much, used too much profanity, engaged in personalities; and if the complaint results in license suspension, don't be one bit surprised!

The Statistics

While you have been reading this chapter—a period of approximately fifteen minutes—135 serious crimes took place in the United States. Nine each minute. In that one fifteen-minute period nineteen people were assaulted, raped, robbed, or murdered. Fifty-six burglaries were committed, twenty-five automobile thefts were completed, and forty-three grand thefts were successfully concluded. In a span of fifteen minutes! Now, multiply that by four times each hour. And multiply *that* by twenty-four hours a day. *Every* day. Now do you know why people are frightened?

Statistics? Yes. Did you ever see a "statistic"? Close up? Lying in the street beaten, broken, bleeding, confused, hysterical? Or weeping and shivering and not to be comforted for the loss of the innocent, smiling world of home and friends shattered forever in a thunderclap moment of vicious injury, unprovoked and undeserved? Or regressing to the safety of childhood, calling for a mother long dead? Or doomed to nightmares and sleeping with a light on in the bedroom as long as life lasts?

Have you ever thought about the terror, the pain, the humiliation, the psychological scars that endure forever that a "statistic" experiences? Or about the financial loss from which a "statistic" never completely recovers? Or about the physical damage and disfigurement which can never be repaired?

Is it possible that, in the course of a year, some statistics might be spared their Gethsemane if municipal governments in general began to take even a limited interest in the qualifications, performance standards, training, licensing, and supervision of security personnel?

Chapter Three

What's a Security Officer Made of?

A Special Kind of Person

THE NATURE of security work is extremely varied and the best security officers are likely to be persons of rather complex nature.

A security officer cannot be like an assembly-line worker who pushes the same button all day long to get the same wedge aligned with the same groove. Such routine work requires no imagination, no initiative, no reasoning, not really much of anything. The most neutral personality in the world can do such a job successfully for forty years and then pick up a pension. Not so the security officer, but let us begin at the beginning.

When you apply for a position as a security officer you will, of course, be expected to have some general qualifications for the job. Because the qualifications are established by the local licensing authority, they vary from state to state and from community to community, and there is simply no way to tell you in advance what they will be.

Some general requirements are always present. For example, you must be able to read and write the English language. (If you also have command of another language it is a big *plus* for you.) You must be a citizen of the United States. You must be able to follow written and spoken orders, and hopefully you can think and act without panic in emergencies.

Many of the requirements, however, are variable. Age is at present a negligible factor, although usually you will have to be at least twenty-one years old. This holds true despite the favorable experience of police departments which have successfully used a lower minimum age.

Just as maturity of and by itself should not be, and at present usually is not, a bar to entry into security work, neither should youth, of and by itself, be a bar to entering security work. Inexperience is inexperience at any age, and inexpertness in performing a security function can be displayed by a security officer at any age. Failure to recognize and take action in a specific situation does not necessarily result from either youth or maturity; it results as often from never having faced a comparable situation as it does from any "age" involved.

Height and weight? No problems here. There is a broad range of acceptable maximums and minimums. It is common practice simply to require that the weight of an applicant be in proportion to height, with so many pounds, more or less, for each inch of height.

Slowly receiving official attention is the fact that many present employment standards were established long ago and are overripe for revision. (What medical examiner bothers taking chest expansion any more?) Today's job applicants are commonly taller and broader and heavier than their parents were, but they are often measured by physical standards set up generations ago.

Hearing and vision? You are expected to have acute hearing and eyesight, but corrections (hearing aid and/or glasses) are permitted and accepted. With corrections (that is, with the assistance of a helping device if a helping device is necessary) or without corrections you are expected to have vision acute both for distance and for close reading. You are expected to be able to hear and understand with either ear ordinary conversation from a distance of fifteen feet.

You must, of course, be able to distinguish and identify basic colors. In other words, if you are color blind, you cannot get a license as a general thing.

Have you been active in sports? Good! While such is not a qualification, private security often requires a degree of physical fitness greater than that needed in many livelihoods, and a record of participation in sports is in your favor. In any event, you will probably be expected to have a successful physical examination prior to acceptance.

You may be married or single. There may be some residence requirements to meet. Ancient common law said that a year of residence made an inhabitant out of a newcomer but, depending on where you live in this country, the residence requirement for security employment may range from three months in the community (and at least a year in the state) to five years in the community. Residence requirements are today coming under considerable fire. Rooted in antique ordinances never repealed, such requirements are often ignored by a community seeking a chief of police or city administrator, and there seems little reason or justice in holding security personnel to such restrictions.

It is possible you will have to take a written examination, although many organizations today rightly consider that when you have completed their formal Application for Employment you have taken a written examination.

You may have to appear before a group of persons who meet regularly to interview applicants. This "oral examination," where the members of the group ask questions and you answer them, is often much easier and more informal than a written examination, so do not let such a requirement disturb you a bit.

Because your personal characteristics such as honesty, dependability, and respect for law are so important in this kind of work, you must expect to have your backgrounds—school, employment, military, health—investigated. A careful job will be done.

You will be fingerprinted. The prints will be sent to the Federal Bureau of Investigation at Washington and to the police departments of cities where you have lived or worked. If you are lucky enough to be applying for security work in a place that really cares about its security officers, you may be interviewed personally by a representative of the police department and photographed there.

Be glad for these things. They set you apart and prove what we repeat over and over in these pages: You are someone special.

Once you are accepted for licensing, some things are sure: You must be willing to accept whatever legal assignment your employer gives you. You must routinely hold yourself ready for emergency service twenty-four hours a day. You have the right and the authority (1) to go armed during your hours of duty on the premises to which you are assigned, (2) to transport your weapon to and from your place of work and your place of residence by the most direct route and (3) to make arrests and conduct searches during your hours of duty, and at the place of your assignment, under the same circumstances as does an officer of the local police department.

Most other things are variables: You may have to be bonded, which means that someone—you or your employer—must put money aside to make good any damage or loss an action of yours may cause. A valid driver's license in force is a convenience. You may be called upon to drive a motor vehicle from time to time. If your driver's license has lapsed and reinstatement will cause you no more trouble than taking the necessary tests, why not reinstate the license?

Just so there is no misunderstanding or disappointment, keep a few things generally in mind: If drinking or the use of drugs, on or off the job, has caused you trouble, or if you have been confined in any sort of mental institute, you will probably have difficulty obtaining a security officer's license. If you have been convicted of a felony or done penitentiary time for one, you will probably have difficulty in obtaining a security officer's license.

Take Alan for an example. He was in his midtwenties and would probably have made a good security officer. He applied for a license, and his record check showed that he had once been convicted of, and received a suspended sentence for, carrying a concealed weapon. It was the one black mark on his record, but the fact remains that he was a convicted felon in the eyes of the law, and there was not any way he could get a license to carry a gun.

As the licensing officer put it to him in the interview which dashed Alan's hopes, "We are not prepared to license felons yet in this state and that is what—according to the definition of law— you are. As such, and according to the Gun Control Act of 1968 you could go to jail for two years just for having a gun on you, and there is not any way we can say, 'You have been convicted of a Federal offense, so we're going ahead anyway and license you to do the very thing you've already been convicted of doing illegally.' No way!"

There was another man—a mature man—who came up for licensing about the same time as Alan. A background investigation revealed that back home many years before, at a time and place in our history when such activity was socially accepted, financially rewarded, and morally endured, he had done some bootlegging and operated an illegal still. He had been taken into custody, tried, convicted, and sentenced. He served one year. When his application for a security officer's license was refused he could not believe it.

"That was thirty *years* ago!" he protested. "I ain't done nothin' since."

And he was telling the truth. He had never been in trouble before or since. He had held his most recent employment for 26 years until the business was absorbed in a merger. The licensing officer was sympathetic, but felonies and firearms do not mix, at least not in the person of a modern security officer, and there was not a chance of the man's being licensed.

On duty and off, it is necessary for you to display the highest standards of personal appearance and conduct, and the disciplined self-control expected of the best lawmen. It is true of security officers just as surely as of police officers that it takes more than a uniform, a club, a badge, and some muscle to make a good officer. Just as regularly and naturally as you take to your assignment, your badge, and flashlight, and sidearm, you must also take your moral and spiritual equipment, your common sense, your patience, and your courage. You must take them because in the process of protecting persons and property against the unruly, the treacherous, and the deranged, you will have need as well to be a helper to the sick, the injured, the lost, the confused, and the inarticulate. And because sooner or later you will meet every twisted personality in your territory, including some like the Budapest brothers who severely beat a police officer and a security officer because "they [the lawmen] put the evil eye on us and turned themselves into cats and cows at night."

You will have to face temptation from those who will try to bribe you to let them escape when you have taken them into custody, and you will have more than one opportunity to betray your employer, to steal, and to permit others to steal. Do not grow careless just because you go along for a while without giving in.

Manny Morton was on one beat for forty years, picking up new clients, making friends, building a reputation. One night as he was inspecting the interior of a gas station, just as he had done a thousand nights before, he saw an open cash box on the desk, with a one-hundred-dollar bill in full view. To the day he dies, Manny will not be able to explain why he did it, but he took the bill, put it in his pocket, and then locked the cash box and stored it in the desk. A police officer on the corner saw Manny in the gas station, just as he had seen him there and in other places since rookie days. The officer thought no more about it until the owner of the gas station complained about the loss of the money. Then the officer remembered and mentioned the circumstances to his sergeant. There was an investigation and they talked to Manny, and Manny is not in security anymore.

Stay out of security if your attitude is "How much can I get and how little can I do in exchange for it?" Once, the field of private security was full of employees with that attitude, and those employees held back the profession intolerably. They still hold it back wherever they are employed, keeping the salaries of security officers low and the morale lower. But private security is today fighting to free itself from such parasites, and is each year hesitating longer before hiring anyone suspected of that attitude. The applicants who today are finding a warm welcome are those who want to make law enforcement and crime fighting their life's work.

Above all, avoid becoming indebted to any person. The acceptance of gifts or favors, no matter how small or how well deserved, can ruin a lawman. There is no way to keep such things secret; and when they become known, there is nobody who believes you are not on the take—including the man who gave you the gift or did you the favor! He will be around to collect, one day, never fear.

If you are a modest man, and most security officers are modest men, you may be tempted to put this book aside, saying, "It's no use. I haven't all these qualities." Probably you do not. Few men or women have all of them. We have been talking ideals, and few humans are ideal. But in every security officer, man or woman, there is a touch of idealism and a dedication to helping people.

Obviously you are idealistic enough to want to make the world a better—or, at least, safer—place than you have found it, or you would not be reading this book. So do not put away your interest in this profession simply because of a printed list of qualifications.

These paragraphs have merely been saying that the work is getting harder and the standards are getting higher, but for men and women who can come even close to meeting the basic qualifications it is a wonderful field in which to work. So follow your star. All the percentages are in your favor. There is no one factor, the lack of which in an applicant dooms him to rejection. It is the total *You*—your attitude and enthusiasm and all your other personality traits, wanting to join in the task of law enforcement —that counts.

There is room for you.

You will make it all right.

Education—How Much?

Let us face it: as the years pass, worthwhile employment is getting harder and harder to obtain with less than a high school diploma or its equivalent.

Law enforcement is rapidly becoming a scientific vocation, in which formal education and professional training in use of the latest devices, implements, developments, and resources of science substitute more and more for the "muscle" which was long considered the chief requirement of a law enforcement officer.

In police circles there appears to be a growing belief that formal education makes better officers in proportion to its amount. Job descriptions are beginning to require x number of years of formal education, into and through college level, for such-and-such a position in the department, or so-and-so many hours of college work before you can take a promotional examination.

Whether or not this is to be considered a good thing depends on whom you talk with. There are thoughtful and experienced police administrators who are convinced that education offers distinct advantages to the officer and his department. Such administrators claim, and no doubt rightly, that better reports are written by educated officers, that the educated officer is usually easier to discipline, understands better what evidence he must supply to make a case, is a better witness, and in general handles himself better in public. Despite the fact that equally strong arguments can probably be presented for the other side, police departments today generally insist that applicants be high school graduates. Applicants with some college training are encouraged, and in more than one city, some college training is required before an applicant will even be considered. In view of this trend, security agencies can hardly afford to hire stupid, dishonest, incompetent, or uneducated personnel. Security officers cannot afford to *be* stupid, dishonest, incompetent, or uneducated. There is no way to avoid the fact that performance cannot and will not rise above the level of intelligence of the officer.

What can education do for you? For one thing, it can give to others a pretty good idea of how smart you are, how teachable you are, and how well you can learn from the experiences of others. Learning from the experiences of others is what you do when you study a textbook. It is what you are doing as you read this page.

The availability of mass education brings you into contact with a better-educated public, and if you are not prepared to deal with this better-educated public, you will have a rough road to travel.

If you are still in high school and have any choice of the subjects you take, give all the time possible to American history, civics, all aspects of spoken and written English, typing, and shorthand. If you are accepted into some areas of private security with less than a high school education, one of two things is bound to happen: Either you will find yourself forever mired in your employer's cat-and-dog assignments, or your employer will let you know he would like to see some signs of ambition in the form of efforts to obtain a high school diploma.

Since it takes years for an educated man to master the complexities of law enforcement work, just how much chance do you think an undereducated person has? If you did not get good grades in English when you were a student, do you think you can prepare reports that will hold up in court? If you have never been much of a reader, how will you read and understand Federal laws, state statutes, city ordinances, security manuals, and law enforcement magazines?

If you feel that you may not today have the education to make it in security, should not you be thinking about night school courses, vocational schools, junior colleges, adult extension divisions, church-sponsored courses, and public courses offered to citizens by some municipal departments and conducted in the city hall, the council chambers, or the armory?

In a way, having an education is like having money. If you have it, everybody can tell. It shows. It stands out, and you do not have to say a word. Moreover, nobody cares at all where you got it or how you got it.

The Personality of a Security Officer

This is no job for a spiritually little man. Little men are or become watchmen, and the damage they do to the image of the security officer is substantial. Why? Because the tendency of such men to unwarranted harshness, capricious arbitrariness, and petty tyranny weakens public confidence and reduces public respect as quickly as does obvious stupidity, dishonesty, or laziness. Personal likes and dislikes have no place in the security officer's professional life; self-discipline and self-control must be his daily and nightly companions.

Responsible security work requires a substantial amount of versatility. It is unnecessary, and probably impossible, to select personality and character traits in any order of importance. Among the qualities important to a security officer we would certainly find *alertness.* It is this quality, perhaps more than any other single attribute, which will determine his effectiveness. It should be cultivated by every security officer. For example, even though hundreds of contacts are completed with individuals who show proof of the right and the need to enter a restricted area, the officer on duty could easily have contact with *one* person who should not enter. To be able to detect this one exception, the security officer would have to be constantly on the watch for warning deviations from the normal. He cannot tell ahead of time the form such warning deviations will take. Perhaps it will be nothing more than controlled nervousness on the part of a person approaching from a direction not generally used, but the officer must spot all such things because little things that would have no significance if taken alone can often add up to something important.

To a security officer *courage* is imperative and *tact* is indispensable. In his task of protecting property and personnel he is society's shield against the rowdy and the vandal. His unending responsibility is to support and enforce the law, and he must preserve order wherever and whenever disorder threatens.

Another helpful characteristic for a security officer to have is the *ability to reason deductively.* By this we mean the ability to look at a given situation and be able to figure out step by step how it came to take place. Take for example the case of two men who entered an apartment in an officer's territory and beat to death a husband and wife for two dollars in the woman's purse. If the security officer knows his job and his neighborhood, he might substantially shorten the police department's apprehension time by trying to think where such creatures came from, how they got into the area, where they would go to hide, and who would know about them.

Still another desirable trait for an officer is the ability to talk to all kinds of people. Just imagine the different classes of people who would have to be approached in a search for the scraps of information which, when put together, could add up to an identification. How can a security officer hope to talk to people of different ages and backgrounds and attitudes toward lawmen if he does not have the knack of putting himself—at least to some degree—in their shoes? Yet some officers never seem to learn that you cannot and do not talk to a company employee, a teen-age shoplifter, a riverfront stray, a two-time loser, a terrified illiterate, and a High Point surgeon in exactly the same way. Those who do not, cannot, or will not learn this are never going to became very good lawmen.

It is, at the very least, expensive and annoying to employers to find out, after they have hired a man, that he cannot even direct an automobile off the company parking lot without having to fight the driver!

These qualities—alertness, courage, tact, the ability to reason deductively, and the ability to talk to all types of people—will take you a long way and will enable you to act on your own decision, in instances where no exact orders have been given to you, without constantly looking for someone else to tell you what your decision should be. These qualities will enable you to exercise your authority fully, firmly, and fairly; to keep your poise and your temper in the face of mindless criticism from your inferiors; and to perform your duties with firmness despite fear, determination despite danger, and patience despite provocation.

If you do not especially like people, and the idea of courtesy and fairness for all does not exactly enchant you, you may have plenty of reason for this feeling. But all the same you can make your professional path a lot easier by use of unvarying courtesy and fairness—the courteous approach and obvious fairness you exhibit to all regardless of age, sex, race, color, creed, oddities of dress, or degree of personal friendship.

The Guilty Bystanders

Unfortunately you are going to see people pretty much at their worst. Even some basically decent, well-meaning, entirely law-abiding citizens tend to get emotional when approached by a uniformed officer. There are those who cannot even ask street directions of an officer easily, and a quiet steady manner is indispensable to you.

As for those that are not basically decent or well-meaning or even humane, you will see their cars lined up for a mile along the highway where a school bus has gone over an embankment and burst into flames. Smoke and the screams of injured children mingle sickeningly in the air. The law officers have a hard time getting help and ambulances to the trapped victims because of the people swarming over the area. What are the people doing?

They are going *Ooooh* and *Ahhh* and quarreling among themselves over the choicest spots for picture taking.

Imagine a street scene in the dead of night in the middle of winter, with nobody moving so far as the eye can see. A fire engine passes the corner, or cars collide, or a fight breaks out on the block. Instantly people seem to spring up out of the ground. They come from under rocks, up from sewers, down from trees. They step from helicopters and arrive on surfboards and the whole area—moments before as lonely and as desolate as outer space—is alive with staring, slack-jawed humanity. It is not that these people are hoping to see someone in tragic trouble or screaming in pain. They just do not want to miss it in case anybody *is*.

The innocent bystanders! You will never be free of them. On your plant parking lot a man is blown to bits by a bomb placed in his car. Do you think you will be the first on the scene? Not a chance! People with cameras will be there before you. People with children [*"Look at the man got blowed up! See, there's a hand!"*] will be there before you. People with rights [*"Don't tell me to move on. This here now is a public place!"*] will be there before you.

If you want to know about people, and what to expect from them, ask the police officer who, moonlighting as a taxi driver, picked up three passengers in the early hours of a Saturday morning. The cab had not moved ten yards before one of the passengers had a knife at the driver's throat and a second passenger was pressing a gun to his head, demanding money. The officer, knowing that if the passengers ever saw his wallet with his badge in it they might well kill him, swung the cab onto the sidewalk and into the plateglass window of a clothing store. With the glass crashing and tinkling around him he rolled out the door on the driver's side, pulled his gun, and got the drop on the trio. The nearest street light was half a block away. He ordered the three to place their hands flat against the wall and then, alone in the dim light, he waited. Cars passed in the street, slowed curiously, and then continued on their way. He called to them and they sped away. Pedestrians passed and he identified himself as an officer and asked them to call the police. They turned their faces away and crossed to the other side of the street, where they stopped and stood and stared. Not one person offered assistance. Not one person walked to a telephone and called the operator. Not one person said, "My name is such-and-such, Officer. What can I do to help?" After twenty minutes the officer's ordeal ended when two mobile patrol officers in an unmarked car passed by, spotted the tableau, and came to his aid. The officer, since that ugly night, has not been quite so warm a person. His first words to his brother officers, after the prisoners were cuffed and on their way, explains what happened to him: "Nobody wanted to help me," he said, scarcely believing, "I felt like crying."

It may sustain you in some similar situation, if right now you get used to the idea that the moment you recite the oath and pin on that badge you become a lonely man. In that uniform you are a Target. You are the Law. You are Authority, and people do not like Authority. They do not even like the authority of a red traffic light and would ignore it if they did not fear getting hit by a car. In the middle of the night, when the danger of getting hit by a car is less, they *do* ignore it. If you let people bother you —with their pettiness, their nosiness, their callousness, their messiness, and their sometimes suicidal stupidity—they are going to get to you sooner or later and irritate you into some action you will always regret.

One of them finally got to Security Officer Ossie Prahston one afternoon, and before the incident finally ended Prahston's license was revoked.

Partly it was Prahston's temperament. He was a bit inclined to take personally things which were not so meant, and doing his job well was less important to him than was the approval of people. On the other hand, the individual who finally pushed him over the edge of endurance had been a thorn in his side for years —always watching Prahston with a patronizing, contemptuous smile, master of the snide jeer delivered gravely and earnestly, source of endless sly, degrading comments muttered to a group of street-corner loafers just within Ossie's hearing.

When the break came, the climax built swiftly. Officer Prahston observed the subject, Braklaus by name, enter a pawnshop on the street and attempt to pawn some articles. The pawnbroker refused to deal and Braklaus came out of the shop, the articles in a brown paper bag. Prahston stopped him (though he had no reasonable grounds to stop and search) and demanded to see what was in the bag. Braklaus refused to tell Prahston what was in the bag and refused to let him search the bag. He bluntly told Prahston to go to hell, walked away, and entered a nearby tavern.

Prahston stopped a passing police officer, voiced to the officer his suspicions of the man and the contents of the paper bag, and went with the officer into the tavern.

Inside, the police officer identified himself to Braklaus, asked for and received permission to examine the contents of the bag. In the bag he saw three transistor radios, not new and claimed as his own by Braklaus, and a cloth bag containing an undetermined amount of small change, silver and pennies, which Braklaus claimed he had removed from a bank at home to pay a bill. In these items the officer found nothing incriminating. He thanked Brakdaus for his cooperation and sent the man on his way.

Completely unsatisfied by this turn of events, Prahston insisted that the officer detain Braklaus on suspicion of theft. Since Prahston was thus making a complaint, the officer went to telephone for a police car. Prahston followed Braklaus, who had started across the street.

On the far sidewalk Prahston once again stopped Braklaus, saying, "I want to see what you have in that bag." Once again Braklaus refused, saying, as was later testified, "You couldn't search me on the street, you couldn't search me in the tavern, and you ain't gonna search me now!" And he pushed past Prahston to walk away.

Enraged past sensible thought, Prahston yelled, "Are you trying to get smart with me?" and raised his nightstick.

The police officer, coming out of the tavern after calling for a cruiser, saw Prahston strike Braklaus several times about the neck and shoulders. Instantly a crowd gathered and the officer, racing across the street, prayed for swift arrival of the cruiser as he called into play every ounce of professional know-how he possessed to keep the crowd under control.

Braklaus, on the spot, called for the arrest of Prahston for unjustified and unprovoked attack, and the police officer had two prisoners when the cruiser arrived shortly thereafter. Meantime Prahston had been advised of his rights. He refused to make a statement.

Braklaus was taken to a hospital where he was treated for a laceration of the nose and contusions of the shoulder and upper arm and released to police custody.

Braklaus' property was not touched at any time by Prahston. Braklaus' wife and sister, contacted at the Braklaus address, described the items in Braklaus' possession, and later came to the police station and verified the identification.

The property of Prahston, including nightstick, badge, handcuffs, gun, cap-piece, ID card, and six rounds of ammunition, was held at the police station.

A criminal information sheet was applied for and next morning the prosecuting attorney's office issued a warrant against Prahston charging assault with intent to do great bodily harm.

Although the case dragged on for months, there was not much that could be done for Prahston. Beyond a personal antipathy to Braklaus, which may well have been more than justified, Prahston had no basis for arrest, no basis for search, and therefore no basis for restricting Braklaus' movements or using force to compel him to submit to an unwarranted search.

Prahston had rejected the police officer's evaluation of the situation although he well knew that participation of a security officer in any incident where police officers are present is limited to identifying himself and offering his assistance.

The mere exchange of heated words between two long-time enemies provided no basis for an attack by Prahston, a security officer on duty, on Braklaus. The Committee of Supervisors recommended that the license of Security Officer Prahston be revoked and it was so ordered.

Your Chances for Employment

Your chances for obtaining employment in private security are excellent. Private security is in a period of tremendous expansion, and career possibilities are becoming steadily greater. Prophecy borders on folly, but the need for qualified security officers is not being met, and the demand will probably exceed the supply for years to come. From conservative estimates, guarded forecasts, and calculations projected well into the future, some fifteen thousand job opportunities each year may be expected to open up in private security. How will this come about? Here is an example of how it will come about: For years friction and irritation and sometimes outright antagonism resulted whenever a local businessman could not immediately obtain for his property the protective police services he thought his tax bill should guarantee. When he then turned to a protection agency and hired guards to patrol his premises, it was interpreted by the local department as criticism of, and dissatisfaction with, its performance. Now the situation has changed. Now it is the police department that suggests to a businessman that he consider supplementing his premises protection by hiring the services of a private protection agency.

In effect the local department is saying that while it certainly will supply all possible protection, there is nonetheless a point beyond which it cannot provide protective supervision to individual businesses on the scale that the local crime situation logically warrants. If a business is situated in a city's crime corridor, or if it can be proven to be highly necessary to local well-being or community survival, the police will lavish on it all possible attention, manpower, and overtime.

At the same time, it is manifestly impossible for any Chief of Police arbitrarily to say that Business A has right to more police protection that Business B. A police department is responsible for the safety of all the citizens and all the city. It has neither the personnel nor the responsibility to insure the physical safety of every candy store and gift shop in town.

The very location of a business or industry, perhaps squatting on the outer fringe of a community, far removed from any patrol pattern, can make adequate protection difficult; its position in a high-crime area may make it extremely vulnerable to assault; the mechanical devices installed by management may be insufficient, undependable, or badly chosen. No matter. In the day in which we are living, a day when private property needs more protection than most police departments are staffed to provide (if they are to discharge their responsibilities to the rest of the community) the only sensible course for a businessman is to make property protection a standard item in his annual budget.

The officers will apprehend any offender they observe injuring or attempting to injure any piece of private property. Such is their duty. But when, simply because of its size or location, a piece of property would require a large number of officers to protect it adequately, the remainder of the community it not required to sacrifice its own share of police protection so the department can concentrate on a few acres of private enterprise.

If a hospital or a school or a manufacturing plant wants to be sure that its property is free of trespassers, rowdies, and vandals; or if a department store or library wants to protect its customers and visitors from pursesnatchers and thieves, the cost of whatever additional protection the owners believe they need should be a routine budgetary item.

In no way or degree does such action reflect adversely on the competence of the local police department. It merely reveals a sober administrative realization that today business must add its own protective efforts to the efforts of the local police department. From such recognition of responsibility come jobs for security officers.

Unhappily, a steadily larger proportion of our growing population seems to be criminally inclined. Crime statistics soar and problems connected with the control of crime and the apprehension—and *conviction*—of criminals multiply. To cite an example, policing is a relatively—*relatively!*—uncomplicated matter in a business center which is a business center only and where, after business hours, nobody lives and few persons are to be found walking the closed and shuttered streets. When such persons are observed, investigation follows promptly. But where commercialization of a community exists, where apartment complexes rub shoulders with sprawling shopping centers containing business and professional offices open twenty-four hours a day; where the area never sleeps and the comings and going—*legitimate? illegal?* —never end, lawmen all but drown in patrol and protection problems.

The result? Jobs for security officers, who can help keep an observant eye on the flowing human tide. Security officers, no matter what local title they carry, are now employed on a regular basis by business enterprises from airports to zoos. Such officers are responsible for making safe the property, personnel, equipment, records, and classified information of private businesses; and for protecting the general public assembled at various locations and events. Obviously the more of this localized observation, prevention, and control that can be transferred to the keeping of privately licensed security personnel and/or agencies, the more thoroughly can the local police officers discharge their preventive patrol, apprehension, and investigation responsibilities for the entire community.

Cities will continue to grow and their growth predictably will be much swifter than the growth of the police forces protecting them. Someone will be needed to take up the slack in the protection needs of the expanding population. Maybe it will be the privately licensed security officer.

Traffic control, a complex problem, has long been a burden and a vexation to police departments, and it will become more abrasive in the future than it is now. Some police planners wonder if the time may not be ripe to relieve the police of this manpower drain and hand the burden over to a separate (and perhaps subordinate?) group who, under police supervision, would make traffic control their full-time job.

Already private security officers are controlling traffic and patrolling parking facilities on the premises of private employers; already they are enforcing for private employers state laws, local statutes, and company regulations in a way no police officer would possibly have time to do; already they are able to remove from the premises employees wanted on warrant or citation and to do so with a minimum of fuss or delay. Could they be trained to help with the traffic tangles in cities? Some think so.

Many Jobs in Security

Remember that every security agency, even a small one, has many jobs besides patrolling.

There are letters to be written, bills to be mailed, accounts to be posted, applications to be screened, employees to be trained, and all sorts of clerical work to be done. There are assignment sheets to be prepared, contracts to be sold, payrolls to be met, work time to be logged, vehicles to be repaired, interviews to be conducted, emergency jobs to be manned—and all these tasks, in addition to being done, must have supervision.

Accordingly, your chances for work in private security are especially bright if you have a specialized skill or an aptitude which can be developed on the job. In such instances there are few agencies where you will not be welcome. Are you good at figures, typing, interviewing? Some of the larger agencies have openings for bookkeepers, dispatchers, secretaries, typists, accountants, electrical technicians. Do you know anything about photography and darkroom work? Pictures are important evidence in instances of accidents, fires, breaking and entering, flood or vandalism damage.

Even if, while you wait the birthday that will let you meet the minimum age requirement, you must take a job on a part-time basis, do not overlook such a chance to get acquainted with security work. Perhaps you could work for a short time at a fair or sports event and see if you like the work. Offer your help to all the agencies you can reach. Do not be disappointed if some of them will not listen: they are just afraid you will work for them for a while and then trade information about them with their competitors. You may be sure all of them have more office and sales work to do than they can complete. The clerical end of some security operations borders on chaos.

After you have been in private security a little while, you should ask yourself what area of the work you enjoy most. You may find that you do your best work in the area of personal protection. The happiest assignments for you are those that make you responsible for the protection and safety of persons or property against physical threats or actual danger; the guarding of payrolls or valuables in transit; the policing of conventions, stockholders' meetings, reunions, or sports events; providing protection to individuals or residential areas against attacks or trespass.

Or you may decide you would rather work (in uniform or in plain clothes) as an officer doing patrol through stores, hotels, office buildings, business establishments, hospitals, garages, guarding against thieves, shoplifters, purse snatchers, and pickpockets.

If you like animals and can find, or make, an opportunity to work with sentry dogs, you may have the time of your life. Dogs bring problems and if you do not want to groom and take care of a dog in health and in sickness, and work as a team with a dog, stay away from this area of security. But for the man who appreciates a fine, courageous companion on lonely night tours of isolated areas, junk yards, loft buildings, amusement parks, cemeteries, race tracks, riverfront, and the like there is nothing like a well-trained dog to practically eliminate trouble with trespassers, prowlers, vandals, burglars, roaming gangs, and hidden criminals.

It would be unrealistic not to face the fact that some of you, as you get the feel of law enforcement, will leave private security and apply for enrollment in the commissioned police ranks. And why shouldn't you? It works the other way, too. As private security raises its standards and becomes more interesting it is attracting active police officers into doing a little moonlighting. Retired officers who thought they were through with law enforcement forever feel the tug after a few idle months and turn to private security with a working lifetime of law enforcement experience.

Employment opportunities will come because attrition (the process of wearing away or thinning out) is always at work. Men and women leave their security jobs to go to other locations and other fields of work, or they retire and leave their places to be filled by newcomers.

Jobs will be available because the truth appears to be that the crime problem is going to get worse before it gets better and police officers need all the dependable friends they can get. Also, there are always a certain number of borderline employees in private security who will not be retained for five minutes by their employers if more promising applicants come along. Sometimes, but not nearly often enough, these borderline employees manage to get themselves fired, like Koops did.

Koops, a warehouse watchman, brooded all one evening while stretched out on the sofa in the manager's office about how over-worked and underpaid and generally unappreciated he was. As he brooded a thought (if it can be called that) began to form in his brain.

Delighted with his inspiration, he left the sofa and went to work setting the scene which would prove to one and all his re-sourcefulness and bravery in driving off some would-be burglars. First, he cut some strands of the perimeter fence to provide an obvious entry point. Then he knocked out the lights over the front and rear entrances. Then he fired several shots into the building, went in and, from the inside, fired several shots to the outside. Then he put his hat on the ground and fired at it, dent-ing the cap-piece. Then he called the police.

Now, the police have been around a long time, and there are brains in even the smallest law enforcement department these days, so it did not take more than five minutes for the funny smell of this scenario to reach the inquisitive nose of the police lieuten-ant who sped to the scene.

A little talk with Koops, a few gentle questions (like *"How many rounds of ammunition do you generally bring to work?"* and *"How many rounds would you say were fired here tonight?"*) and the story came out. Koops was charged with filing a false re-port and with discharging a firearm within the city limits. His employers felt that they would no longer require Koops' services.

You Can Find a Job

Inevitably, job opportunities in private security are greater in some cities than in others because some cities recognize more clearly than others the potential of this supplementary arm of law enforcement and make an effort to develop it, encourage it, guide it, and support it. Moreover, as crime rates have risen throughout the nation the increase in cities has been substantially greater than in the less-heavily populated areas of the countryside. This holds true for both major categories of crimes, the serious crimes and the petty crimes and misdemeanors. Juvenile delinquency and drunkenness, for example, impose a major drain on the limited time of patrol officers in large cities. In small towns such problems, if and when they come to police attention, are more likely to be handled quickly, informally, and comparatively quietly.

So how do you get a security job? Security agencies and private business organizations alike are advertising aggressively and you should begin to read the advertisements, both classified and display, in your area newspapers.

It can be kept in mind that fewer than 10 percent of security personnel in the United States (those working as security personnel under all the titles attached to this area of employment) are nonwhite. This low percentage seems to indicate that either the members of a vast pool of potential applicants are not aware of, or have failed to think seriously about, employment opportunities in the field. Either way, the result is a loss to law enforcement. Members of so-called minority groups are people. Good, bad, and indifferent people, just like everybody else, and when a member of any such group becomes interested in law enforcement and gets a chance to prove that interest, he tends to perform superbly.

In view of today's rapid urban spread and the influx of millions of people who are strangers to our customs, our ways, our laws, our language (not to mention a native suspicion of law officers), employment of minority group members is becoming a matter of pressing importance. The diversity of non-English speaking peoples in our larger cities, for example, makes it imperative that more security officers be employed who are of such races and are accordingly familiar with their habits, their background, and their motivation.

It is true, of course, that some who are aware of the opportunities, fear that they will not receive fair treatment in pay, assignments, and promotions, or that they will have to arrest their friends, or that their wives and children will be harassed and threatened by the neighbors. These considerations are realistic, and they represent hindrances which each person must evaluate individually. However, the national attitudes of disgust and antipathy toward crime suggest that in many instances these impediments will not prove as substantial as they may at first appear.

In addition to the Help Wanted advertisements, you can learn of opportunities from the office of the state employment service, from the Veterans Administration, from your school placement bureau, from friends and acquaintances already employed in security, from the personnel departments of retail stores, industrial plants, and contract guard and protection services listed in the Yellow Pages of your telephone directory. You can run an advertisement of your own in your local newspaper, offering your services. Or you can hire a private employment agency to find openings for you.

When you present yourself for an interview a conservative appearance is recommended. Employers pay the wages, and employers are conservative, and if you do not at least look conservative you will be put at the bottom of the candidate list and, if hired, may be marked for replacement at the first opportunity. Why impose an unnecessary handicap on yourself?

Hiring procedures vary from one organization or agency to another, but in accordance with what we have already reported in this book, you will—when you apply—either be told or will be handed a printed card which reads: "To be considered for any job with this organization you must be a citizen of the United States. You must possess good moral character and have no unfavorable record of law violations, either convictions or pending charges. If you do not meet these requirements, do not fill out an application because you will not be considered. If you do meet these requirements, fill out the application form carefully, writing or printing the answers in your own hand. Your application must be complete, accurate, and legible for you to be considered." Now give yourself a simple test: Are you able to take a plain blank card and on it provide for an employer, in legible handwriting, your full name, your address with zip code, your social security number, and a telephone number where he can get in touch with you? This is not a joke. You would be surprised, and maybe shocked, at the number of applicants who cannot! If *you* cannot, why? And why should anyone hire a person so incompetent?

If you meet the basic general requirements (which are not at all difficult) and are being considered for an existing opening, you will probably be interviewed immediately. Just remember that no employer *has* to give you a job. The only interest any potential employer has in you is what *you* can do for *him*. He is willing to pay you because he thinks you can give him something he wants very much: a feeling of security when he goes home at night and a good chance that the business he worked a lifetime to build will be there in the morning. That is worth money to him, and it is worth money to you if you can deliver, because never before were there so many chances for an alert, courageous man or woman to provide and sell that precious commodity: security.

Chapter Four

Nothing but the Truth

The Weakest Link

IT IS NOT A matter for argument that training in basic law enforcement procedures is important to the satisfactory performance of security duties. Even the simplest course in methods of crime prevention and control works wonders in increasing the confidence, pride, and effectiveness of a security officer.

Police departments long ago learned that training is vital to the development of quality officers. Security agencies know the same truth but—perhaps because the name of the game is profit—many of them seem reluctant to make the financial investment necessary to train their employees. As a consequence too many security officers remain untrained. They remain untrained not because they are disinterested in training or are incapable of absorbing it but because training is either not required of them or is unavailable to them.*

City administrators commonly respond to any overture in the direction of training by asking bleakly, "Why should we train these people? They aren't city employees. Where would we get instructors? Where would we hold classes? How would we pay for heat and light and secretarial help? Let their employers train 'em!"

There are statements in this book which can be interpreted as advocating that police departments assume training and supervisory responsibility for local private security agencies and personnel. Such advocacy is more apparent than actual, although the idea is sound enough to merit consideration. Police departments may indeed be exactly the logical agencies to handle such activity; equally often they may not be. Sometimes the idea may be impractical for budgetary reasons. Even though many of the expendi-

---

*An attempt to solve the training problem is made in another book by John Peel: *Fundamentals of Training for Security Officers* (Charles C Thomas, Publisher).

tures incident to setting up such a departmental operation would be nonrecurring, the initial budget is generally big enough to discourage official interest. There is, however, more to the problem.

In the comparatively few instances where police departments have undertaken a teaching and supervisory role, Utopia has not resulted. Some dramatic community benefits (a substantially increased measure of mutual respect, trust, and cooperation between the police officers and the security officers, to name one) have resulted, but so have complaints of police intrusion into private enterprise. Refusals by some security organizations to cooperate have resulted. Efforts by protection agencies to bypass, impede, or scuttle the program have resulted.

Police reluctance to move deliberately into such cross fire is scarcely to be wondered at. But regardless of how the problem is viewed, does it seem unreasonable to equate a city's responsibility to protect its citizens with a responsibility to train and supervise persons charged with that protection?

Training is the quickest and best way to get the greatest value out of security officers simply because training makes them better officers. Trained officers can do more, do it better, and do it in less time than untrained officers. Few investments pay off more quickly in greater safety for the people and the property of the community than a compulsory training program for security personnel. However, few communities make any effort to train security officers, to investigate existing performance standards, or to eliminate personnel obviously unfit for their duties. As a result, there are not enough adequately trained persons available to meet the increasing demand for security personnel and protection service, and inexperienced, unfit, even unstable persons are being imposed on clients. Such indifferent, inefficient, incompetent persons stain the reputations of all security officers, debase the security profession, degrade the agencies that assign them as "protection," and annoy the employers and general public they are supposed to serve.

What Do I Do?

As for *you*, what do you do if no opportunity for training exists in the place where you plan to work and make your living? The answer is blunt: you may either move to a place where training is available, or go to work without training.

Much, unfortunately, seems to depend on luck, on where you are when you decide you would like security work. If you are lucky, you may find training immediately available to you, and law enforcement courses obtainable at nearby vocational schools, high schools, junior colleges, or fraternal organizations. If such resources are denied to you, and you are unable to move to a place where they exist, there is a third alternative which is here presented with extreme reluctance and strong warnings to proceed with caution: home study.

Home study courses in various phases of law enforcement are presently available through sources your librarian or supervisor of schools can tell you about. Subjects include police administration, traffic control, patrol, crime prevention, juvenile delinquency, basic law, and others.

However, there is so little regulation or control of mail-order education that you should sign nothing (not even a request for information; *type* your signature) until you obtain a favorable report about the school of your choice from the Better Business Bureau, the Association of Commerce, your school guidance counselor, the superintendent of schools, or the advisor at the state employment office—or better yet, from *all* such persons and service organizations.

The Federal Trade Commission has found that false and misleading statements, implied or actual promises of employment, and outright misrepresentations abound in the advertising and promotional practices of some correspondence schools. Do not forget this fact.

Maybe a study course is not the best solution for you anyway, or at least, not the only solution. Maybe you should think about buying books and subscribing to some law enforcement magazines and starting your own personal security library. Evenings and weekends and even during breaks on your job, have close at hand a magazine or one of the books on security practices which are becoming more numerous and available. If you cannot find anything written especially for security officers on a subject of interest to you, read one of the books written for police officers on that subject. You will be interested and rewarded.

It is precisely because law enforcement work is becoming steadily more demanding that security officers are sharing the responsibilities of commissioned police officers. Methods and equipment are changing rapidly, specialization is becoming more common, and this area of work is no different from others: if you want to progress there is no end to studying, learning, adapting, and changing. In other words, there is no end to training.

If you say that you do not want advancement at such a price and that you will be fully content with a good, steady, modest job that leaves you some time for yourself, you are to be admired. There is indeed much more to life than a headlong race to be the first man in the organization to get an ulcer or have a heart attack.

The Deadly Night

The newspaper story said:

"A security officer was shot to death early this morning on the south parking lot of St. Lucy's Hospital by a man he sought to question. The shooting took place about two o'clock at the height of the snowstorm which blanketed this area to a depth of four inches during the night.

"The slain man, Aneas Godfrey, 42, was employed as a security guard by the hospital, which has been the scene of more than fifty incidents in the past year. He was admitted to St. Lucy's emergency room, where he was pronounced dead on arrival.

"Police, called to the scene by the night supervisor of nurses, followed footprints to a nearby tavern, where they took into custody Bobby Kaerf, 19, of the 7800 block of Paige Street. Kaerf, an ex-convict, had the weapon used in the killing in his possession. The officer's wristwatch was also recovered."

An automobile parked at the scene said:

"He was heavy and limp when he fell against me. He said, 'Oh, God, it's so soon!'."

The security officer's revolver said:

"He didn't call me. I was resting in my holster. I heard him say, 'Who are you and what are you doing here?' And then a loud, round, final sound like I make."

His notebook said:

"I fell in the snow in front of his face. I fluttered my pages at him but he didn't see me!"

The falling snowflakes said:

"We couldn't cover the red."

His killer said:

"He didn't ought to of messed wit' me. He waren't nuthin' but a goddam watchman."

The prosecuting attorney said:

"I've known this creep for ten years. He's got a record as long as your arm. It's all there: truancy, petty theft, auto theft, attempted rape, strong-arming, assault, carrying concealed weapons. Twenty-two bookings. One conviction. Paroled. Now murder."

The defense attorney said:

"This unfortunate young man has been oppressed by a heartless and materialistic society."

The judge said:

"The defendant's confession was illegally obtained and is inadmissible as evidence."

The jury said:

"Not guilty."

The officer's mother said:

"Doesn't anybody care about victims any more?"

A neighbor said:

"Why do judges and juries and juvenile courts set known criminals free?"

His brother said:

"I've bought a gun and I'll *use* it."

His employer said:

"Who keeps turning these bums loose? That Godfrey was a good man. He really kept an eye on things around here."

His eight-year-old son said:

"When it was payday, he used to take me to the store and let

me buy something for my very own self."
His wife said:
"I want him back."

Seldom-Told Tales

Unless you can accept, and adjust your daily actions to, the fact that there are animals roaming the streets dressed like human beings, whose only purpose in life is to injure people and make them suffer, stay out of security.

The following paragraphs present an aspect of law enforcement today. If any reader is lost to private security as a result, perhaps it is just as well.

One of the serious problems security officers face is the general attitude of disrespect for authority however it is clothed—as parent, teacher, law officer, or religion.

The rate of assaults on law enforcement officers in the performance of their duty has been climbing for years and given no hint of leveling off. While every assault does not inevitably result in personal injury, a good 50 per cent of such attacks do result in physical harm to the officer, and to loss of duty time in addition.

Statistics for security officers are not available, but a look at figures assembled by the Federal Bureau of Investigation will give an idea of why veteran police officers say, "It's a jungle out there. I never saw anything like it!"

During one recent ten-year period 561 law enforcement officers —city, county, and state police—were murdered in the line of duty. These were not in any degree accidental deaths; these were *murders.*

The hours of darkness are the most dangerous, of course, and so it will be with you. Nearly three quarters (398 officers, or 71%) were killed between the hours of 4 P.M. in the afternoon and 4 A.M. in the morning. The eight-hour span between 7 P.M. and 3 A.M. has proven the most deadly, with 309 of the officers meeting death at the hands of felons during this period.

Friday is the worst day. More officers were killed on Friday than on any other day of the week. Friday's deadliness was followed in sequence by Saturday, Thursday, Sunday, Monday, and Wednesday. Tuesday was the "safest" twenty-four hours of all.

You will be interested in the most dangerous types of calls. The highest incidence of police officer deaths (193, or 66%) resulted when officers working in one-man patrol cars were attempting to make unassisted arrests or were transporting prisoners. The second most dangerous assignment was interrupting robberies in progress or pursuing suspects—death came to 112 officers this way. The third most dangerous assignment was responding to disturbance calls: a family quarrel, a man with a knife or gun, rowdies. Death came to 107 officers on such calls.

Investigating suspicious circumstances or persons resulted in death for fifty-three officers; interrupting a burglary in progress or pursuing a burglary suspect also resulted in death for fifty-three officers. Forty-three officers lost their lives in ambush or in unprovoked attacks made without warning by deranged or beserk persons.

Two hundred and forty-three of the murdered men died alone and unassisted. The others were receiving assistance from other officers at the time they were killed. Eighty-seven of the murderers were killed at the scene of the crime, or shortly thereafter, by police officers.

Meet the murderers: These 561 officers were killed by 741 known offenders. Three out of four killers (75%) had been arrested on some criminal charge before becoming involved in the police killings. More than half (54%) of those with a prior criminal arrest record had previously been taken into custody for a crime of violence such as murder, rape, robbery, assault with intent to kill, and so on. Twenty-five per cent were on probation or parole when they killed the officer.

Of the 741 individuals who were involved in the police murders, well over half (63%) had prior convictions (that is, they were not merely arrested, but were booked, charged, tried, and convicted) on criminal charges, and of this group, two thirds had been granted leniency in the form of probation or parole in at least one of these prior convictions. Nineteen of the individuals involved in the killing of an officer had been convicted on a previous occasion of the commission of murder. Together they had accumulated an average of four-plus arrests each in an average criminal career of ten years.

There is no way you can identify these people by outward marks or signs. They look like ordinary human beings. Their ages range from thirteen to eighty-two years; fifty of them were under the age of eighteen; six out of ten are white and four out of ten are non-white; the average age is twenty-six.

And there they are, and thousands like them, roaming the streets freely, mingling daily with decent citizens who cannot conceive of such viciousness, decent citizens who do not believe anyone would do them intentional harm, decent citizens who are lambs in a jungle. Your job?

Actively support the police in preventing the slaughter of the innocents.

Neglected Ally

Add to the existence of naked danger in this work, the drawbacks of low wages, long hours, scanty training, inadequate (where they exist at all) sick and injury compensation, nonexistent fringe benefits, and the cost of personal equipment, and you begin to see why private security has recruiting problems.

The business community long ago learned that to attract quality personnel it must offer quality inducements. Private security is a business, a big business, and it is not immune from the same economic law.

Capable men who are attracted to law enforcement work are not one bit attracted to the present rock-bottom level of pay and they will not—given any kind of alternative—tolerate it. There are a lot of men working as security officers today because they would rather be underpaid lawmen than fairly paid anything else, but that is a bit of good luck which should not be pushed too hard or too long.

The unfairness of the present wage scale bites even deeper when it is realized how much of his earnings a security officer must spend toward the purchase and upkeep of his own equipment. He must often pay for his record check, his physical exam-

ination, his training, his license, and his uniform. He must pay
for his gun, his club, his handcuffs and make a deposit for his
badge, cap-piece, and shoulder patch. He must replace or repair
lost or damaged equipment. If he is self-employed as a beat man
he must possess and maintain a car. He may wish to invest in the
purchase, training, and care of a dog. And remember that the
end of the expense does not come with purchase of the equipment. Upkeep must be considered and employers commonly dis-
claim any obligation to assist in equipment care or maintenance.
How many men are able to make this kind of investment in a new
job?

What is the result? If he is one of the determined and dedicated law enforcement candidates that private security needs and
tries to attract, he borrows the money and goes to his job with a
millstone of debt around his neck. This condition may not long
be permitted to continue. It is essential that a security officer be
reasonably free from financial worry. His salary should at the
very least permit decent living standards for himself and his
family.

He should have an annual vacation with pay; sick leave with
pay; illness, accident, and death benefits, and pension provisions
on an actuarial basis. Today provisions to take care of a security
employee or his dependents in the event of his serious illness or
injury are more the exception than the rule.

Ten- and twelve-hour work days will never be attractive to
a security candidate who sees all about him lawmen routinely
working eight-hour days and forty-hour weeks. Forty hours a week
should be the maximum necessary to give a good man a good living. He should not have to moonlight on a second or a third job
to make ends meet.

A security officer's job is not as free of danger, and seldom as
easy, as the job of the average employee in the business community. He should not be required to chafe under the feeling of being unfairly treated, and he should be paid with full recognition
of the responsibilities, hardships, and risks which his service en-
tails.

It is close to being a true miracle that this nation has as many dependable, dedicated security officers on duty day and night as it has. They *have* to be dedicated to law enforcement; certainly it is not the salary that lures them!

You have already been warned that your work "day" may actually begin at any of the twenty-four hours, and that you must hold yourself ready for emergency assignments. Sundays and holidays have only one thing sure about them: you will not get as many with your family as the average man gets. Actually you will find that you have to work the hardest on the days that other people have off. These demands are bound to interfere with your home life and social activities.

You will almost never have a steady work location because you will be transferred from one assignment to another at the direction and the need of your employer. You may be exposed to extremes of weather for long periods to the point where your health may be threatened.

When accidents occur, in a plant for example, you will often be the first one on the scene and you may—despite your best efforts—have to watch a man die.

In this most demanding of professions you are always in the public eye and you may expect to be lied about. The thief whom you catch in the act can be depended on to tell the judge that he was not doing anything, that you arrested him because you have taken a personal dislike to him, that the arrest was accomplished with a brutal display of unnecessary force, that you pulled a gun on him, beat him, robbed him of his money, and framed him by putting reefers in his pocket.

Dangerous and hazardous conditions are a part of your daily life, and of all the problems and challenges you will meet, there are two that will be especially dangerous because you never thought about them and never expected to meet them on your job: loneliness and monotony, the ugly twins. They have ruined and killed more security officers than any other heartless pair the officers ever meet. They torment and trick and confuse and deceive a man, and wear him down if he does not watch out, so he does not think straight, does not see what he is looking at, and does not recognize what he sees.

You will have your victories. Every security officer has some to remember. A burglar apprehended, a credit-card racket shattered, a pickpocket eliminated, a mugger captured, a thief convicted—there are such successes in every protective career. Excepting those occasional high points, there is likely to be little to mark for an officer the days melting into weeks, and weeks melting into months, and months melting into years, if he is good at his job.

This is the very point which is so difficult to sell to a company treasurer when budget and contract discussions come up. How do you place a value on things that do not happen? Yet that is exactly what an employer is being asked to do, and that is exactly the precious product a security officer has for sale: accidents that do not occur; thefts that never take place; fires that do not start; property destruction that vandals never inflict. The daily routine procedures and alertness which result in absence of fires, reduction of crime, and elimination of accidents and vandalism result also in the security officer's highest accomplishment: nothing at all happening when and where he is on duty. Thus, the only way a security officer can measure the scope of his contribution to the safety of his domain, the only way he can estimate how well he has done his job, the only way he can estimate how much grief and loss he has prevented is by having nothing much to remember!

Forget the shootouts. Forget the high-speed chase down the highway. Forget riot duty. Forget the heroic rescue from the blazing building. Those moments may come, but even if they do, they are kid stuff compared to the rocklike steadiness of your daily performance when there has been nobody to know and to applaud. They are flimsy as cobwebs compared to the sheer guts you showed that night your baby was sick, but when the time came and the moment came, you uniformed up and went to your job. They are unsubstantial as dreams compared to the daily performance for which you prepare by getting yourself mentally and physically ready for your job and for the emergency that *might* happen today, though it has never happened before in the history of your employment.

You will earn your pay, never fear. You will earn it by fighting, on your employer's behalf, monotony and loneliness and abuse and indifference. You will earn it by working alone or with others as ordered, for long and irregular hours under emergency conditions, perhaps without relief. You will earn it with hours of standing or walking, indoors or outdoors, in heat, cold, rain, and snow. If you are any good at your job, you will earn it just by being there!

The Good Part

You should think very quietly and seriously about what you have just read, and then you should remember the other side of private security, the good part. There are today very few fields of employment that will welcome you more eagerly and treat you better, in exchange for a little bit of honest effort, attention, and enthusiasm. The work is essential, the duties are significant, there is no manual labor involved, and there are no seasonal layoffs.

As a security officer you are one of the important people in the community. You work in a vital area of employment and have many opportunities for service to your neighbors and to the general public. There is great personal satisfaction in the work, in knowing your own worth, and in knowing the value of your contribution to the safety of the community. You have the respect of all law-abiding people.

Because of the countless aspects of human nature which you meet in your work every day, you will get a free liberal education without even knowing it. You may not get the highest pay in the world, but the rate is steadily improving and meantime you have a job as long as you want one.

You may be—you will be—pressured by many problems but if, one day, you wish to change employers you will quickly find that what you have learned on one job serves you very well on another. The basic rules for good security are fundamental and apply widely; any variations occur in the specialized needs of different employers whose unique requirements can only be learned on the job.

Instructed Ally

Knowing and accepting the darker side of the work as you are now able to do, there will be no unpleasant surprises for you, nor will you ever feel cheated or misled or betrayed. Even formal training is becoming more available every day. Sooner or later your turn will come. It will be something like this:

Grinning, the crisply uniformed police sergeant regards the two-score men seated at both sides of the long tables stretching down the narrow room away from where he stands.

"If stealing under fifty dollars is a misdemeanor and stealing over fifty dollars is a felony, what is stealing exactly fifty dollars?"

Eighty withdrawn, cautious eyes watch him steadily and without expression.

The sergeant's grin widens. He nods amiably.

"Sure it's a loaded question. Who knows the answer? If stealing under fifty dollars is a misdemeanor and stealing over fifty dollars is a felony, what is stealing exactly fifty dollars?"

From the far end of the room a burly guard who has been on duty at a steel mill all the previous night rumbles irritably, "Tidy!"

The sergeant's laugh explodes along with the hoots of the other men in the room, and another training session for privately licensed security officers gets under way at the training academy.

By half past eight each Tuesday morning you can see the men beginning to gather at the gray stone building for the classes.

If the day is mild, they may collect in singles and in groups of twos and threes on the sidewalk outside. If the day is wet or depressing, they will drift inside and climb the twenty-five broad steps to the inviting comfort of the chrome and black leather chairs in the lobby.

Some, working for indifferent or uncooperative employers, come tired from a just-ended night's patrol. Most come with their guard up, though not so many now as in the early days of the city's program. All, even the most cynical and suspicious, soon thaw under the relaxed informality of the instructors, who are the same officers who regularly train the city's police recruits.

In the course, which includes four days in the classroom and one day on the pistol range, no theory is preached and no civilian instructors are used. The practical, down-to-earth instruction is given by officers seasoned by many years out on the street. It is not uncommon to have a classmember nod quiet approval to an instructor's comment and say to the man next to him at the table, "He's been there all right!"

There is frank realization that the hairsplitting arguments about degrees of crime and guilt which good-humoredly erupt from time to time could be suicidal nonsense if indulged in by a man alone at two o'clock in the morning investigating a broken window in a high-crime area. The fact that state law says it is not a felony until "the value of the property stolen is at least fifty dollars" is not of immediate importance to a solitary security officer who comes on a pack of teen-age animals looting a vending machine or sacking a schoolroom.

"The procedures we teach you are sound," trainees are told, "but they are not eternal or infallible. They are guidelines for you so long as they serve your needs, but let mature common sense prevail over rules."

Classmembers hear a towering patrolman say, "Look, I'm paid to protect public life and property. You are paid to protect private life and property. That's the only difference between us."

Actually, there are other differences, as the classmembers learn. A police officer, for example, is a police officer twenty-four hours a day, always possesses his powers of arrest, search, and seizure, and always goes armed. The privately licensed security officer is a law enforcement officer only during his hours of duty, and only at the place specified in his license, and thus may go armed and make legal arrest and searches only at such times and places.

At this point a storm of discussion invariably breaks over the instructor's head. He is bombarded with protests from security officers who have been threatened, trailed, and attacked after leaving the location of their assignment. Story after story is brought out to prove how often the security officer takes prompt and courageous action outside his hours of duty and away from the place of his assignment.

The instructor hears about Security Officer Roche, who had just arrived at his place of duty and was parking his car when he saw a youth tampering with a parking meter. As he approached, the youth's accomplice yelled a warning and the youth began to run. Officer Roche caught him after a short chase, placed him under arrest, and held him for police. A master parking meter key, two meter coin boxes, four dollars in nickels, and a nickel-plated revolver were taken from the youth, who implicated his lookout. Warrants charging theft were issued against both subjects.

The instructor hears about Security Officer Boyland, employed by a local security agency. Boyland, off duty and in civilian clothes, saw a newsstand vendor assaulted. He went to the aid of the victim, whose assailants fled. The victim was able to furnish a good description of the three. Boyland called police, gave them the descriptions, waited while they further questioned the victim, and joined them in searching the area. The three assailants were arrested a few minutes later, and positively identified by the victim. Robbery warrants were issued against all three subjects.

The story of Security Officer Oscar Neal is brought out. Neal was on his way home one evening when he saw three juveniles push a woman to the pavement and snatch her purse. Almost on reflex, Neal curbed his car, jumped out, and went in pursuit. He captured two of the hoods—one fourteen years old, one fifteen years old—and held them for the police and turned them over when the officers arrived. The purse was recovered and returned to the victim, who was transported to a hospital in a police cruiser where she was treated for abrasions of knee and elbow.

The instructor, knowing that these trainees have no wish in the world except to be good law officers, listens patiently to stories he has heard before and knows what he will have to say as long as the statutes remain as they read today.

He says, "I know some of these men personally and they are brave men. Oscar Neal is a friend of mine and I was one of the officers that took those teen-age hoods from his custody after that incident happened, but he still took a chance. Oscar *knows* that these purse snatchers work in gangs. If one or two or three punks snatch purses in an area, they already have an escape route planned, and along that route there are other punks waiting to harass anybody giving chase. They are bully-boys, frequently armed and always trigger-happy, and Neal must have known what a chance he was taking."

"Yeah but," the story teller insists, "he cleared eight burglaries, a robbery, a larceny, five purse snatchings, and God knows how many attempted snatchings."

"What you say may be true——," the instructor begins.

"May, hell! *Is* true!"

"*Is* true," agrees the instructor with a smile, "but he still had no more authority than any citizen. Think for a moment about what might have happened to any of these men, or to any of you, if things didn't fall just right. Suppose, on the one hand, the subject resisted to the point where you, in self defense had to club him into submission. He or somebody representing him sues you for injuries sustained. And don't think this sort of thing doesn't happen. It happens all the time! Who is going to pay your legal fees? And if the judgment goes against you, who will pay the damages assessed against you by a jury that hates lawmen?

"Or look at it another way: Suppose the subject is too much for you to handle and injures you, and you require extensive hospitalization. Or suppose you are shot or knifed so that you'll never work again. Who is going to pick up the hospital bill? The rehabilitation costs? Support you and your dependents and pay medical bills for the rest of your life? The citizen you rescued? Don't bet on it! The agency that employs you? You were not on duty! The company to which you were assigned? They have no obligation to you.

"So it's considerations like these that lie behind our recommendations that you think twice before becoming involved in police action when you don't have police authority. I do not say it is right, and I know there are growing sentiments for change. All I am saying is that's the way the law is now and you should keep it in mind."

The instructor falls silent and feels the resentment in the room. It is never easy for lawmen to hear that their city trusts them only for eight hours out of every twenty-four. And the instructor, hoping he has made a point, even though his class tries stubbornly to tune him out, hears a man about halfway down the room begin:

"I was out at Deer and Easton one Sunday morning—just at that time of false dawn when things are visible but not *very* visible—I was driving on my beat when I saw this guy running down an alley with a tire and a wheel.

"I swung across the street and poked the nose of the car into the alley and, sure enough, up ahead in the lights there's this guy going down the alley with a tire fully blown up and on a wheel. Well, I pulled up alongside him and said something like: 'Would you come over here a minute, sir. I'd like to talk to you.'

"He came over to the car and dropped the wheel to the ground, puffing hard.

" 'What are you doing with that wheel? It's pretty heavy, I should think?'

" 'Well, a friend of mine had a flat tire and I just had it fixed and was bringing it back to him.'

" 'Fixed?' (*At dawn? On Sunday morning?*) 'Didn't he have a spare?'

" 'No, sir. He never did have a spare.'

" 'Well, look. Get in and I'll drive you over. Where is your friend's car?'

"He thought for a moment.

" 'Oh. Well, I don't mind taking this the rest of the way. It's only a couple of blocks over there.'

"I suspected I wasn't getting the truth, but I didn't have enough to make an arrest. So I said, 'Get *in!* I've got the time and there's no need for you to carry that big wheel and tire over.'

"So he got in and directed me to where his friend's car was supposed to be. There was no car to be seen in any direction, but he wouldn't give up. When I asked him, 'This is the place? Where's the car?' he answered, 'He must of drove off!' and I arrested him on the spot. I had asked him if his friend had a spare tire and he said there was no spare. His friend may have driven off in a car with three workable wheels, but I was going to listen to that explanation at the station house!"

The class waits expectantly, but the instructor merely nods

and, without comment, picks up the subject matter of the class session. In the back of his mind, however, and never to be wholly eradicated, lurks the knowledge that to these men, in the highest tradition of the best police officers, law enforcement is not a part-time hobby. It is their whole life. He finds himself wishing that each of his brother police officers could work with a class like this for a while. They might begin to realize that in a university or hospital complex, or in a housing project, or in a city park in the middle of the night a well-trained, resourceful private patrolman is, or can be, an ally rather than a competitor, an asset rather than a liability. That here, in fact, are men and women *worth* training, men and women who are eager to be cooperative police supporters in a day when regard for law and order and discipline and consti-tuted authority seems to be vanishing.

A cross section of the private security profession can be seen at each training class. There will be black hair, white hair, red hair, brown hair, and no hair. Ages will be from twenty-one up. There will be security officers, male and female, from national and local protection agencies, banks, hospitals, hotels, public utilities, manu-facturing companies, trucking and transportation lines, depart-ment stores, and retail chains. There will be novices who have yet to receive their first assignment, and there will be veteran officers who were prowling docks and wharves when today's instructors were entering grade school. There will be all varieties of dress—from brisk business suits to freshly pressed uniforms, from sweat-ers and skirts to wild sport shirts. There is not a class without its sprinkling of former police officers who found that their pro-fessional skills did not carry over 100 percent into the field of private security and are accepting a chance to brush up.

Course content ordinarily includes, but is not necessarily limited to, instruction in the authority and responsibility of se-curity personnel, an introduction to criminal law, warrant ap-plications and court procedure, crime scene investigation and protection, evidence identification and preservation, first aid, patrol and crowd-control techniques, care and safe handling of firearms.

The instructors consider that they are training other law en-

forcement officers and treat the trainees accordingly. They tell
stories on themselves they have never told before except among
their own. The security officers, as a result, take to the sessions
like rain to a newly washed car and when their enthusiasm is
added to the over all high quality of the instruction, there is a
positive cooperative crime-control venture going in town.

Candidates for a license who miss sessions cannot be certified
and are advised to apply for enrollment in the next class.

There may or may not be a charge for the instruction. If there
is a charge it can be paid by the trainee or by his employer. When
the course is successfully completed, the trainee receives a certificate and his employer is notified.

The last day of training ends with a brief impressive cere-
mony. The class members meet one final time in the classroom,
by now familiar and comfortable, and renew the oath they took
when they were first licensed:

> "*I do solemnly swear . . . diligently and faithfully . . . without partial-
> ity or prejudice . . . discharge my duties according to the Constitution
> of the United States, the laws of the State . . . and the statues of the
> City . . . and comply with the lawful rules, regulations, and orders of
> the Department of Police . . . So help me God!*"

Then in alphabetical order each man's name is called and he
moves forward to receive his certificate, attesting his successful
completion of the training course, and signed by the Chief of
Police and the Director of Training.

Suddenly it is over. The men are free to go back to their
hard, lonely, thankless, dangerous jobs. They leave the classroom
almost absentmindedly and wander into the lobby where for days
they have sipped scalding coffee from plastic cups and argued
about professional problems. They look around and recall the
names, unknown a week ago, of instructors they will never forget.
They move down the broad marble steps and push through the
double glass doors out into Main Street.

Somehow the city does not look so tough tonight.

Tough enough, but it can be had. Because they are not alone
anymore. They have made friends downtown with their own kind.

They are lawmen, by God!

And so are you.

Chapter Five

Some Faces of Security

Some Duties Do Not Change

IN THIS CHAPTER we shall look at several different areas of private security and examine, insofar as space permits, their special requirements, duties, advantages, and, occasionally, drawbacks.

Any such overview has its hazards. Compression is a necessity and much of the material is inconstant by nature. Times and needs and policies change. Techniques, which often are no more than reflections of the accumulated knowledge of the men in the jobs, change when the men change. Employment statistics and job requirements differ from state to state, company to company, job to job, month to month.

As a result, some material of importance (specific information concerning pay rates, for example, or number of jobs available, or sections of the country with the greatest employment opportunities, or position requirements) may be reported only in the broadest terms, or even omitted entirely.

Nevertheless, the chapter will serve to demonstrate the wide range of security employment possibilities and will underscore the fact that wherever you work in private security, many of your basic duties and responsibilities remain the same.

You patrol to protect life and property, to prevent crime, to preserve the peace, to enforce laws and ordinances, and to apprehend violators. Your concerns include the furniture, stairs, railings, floors, skylights, ceilings, doors, windows, platforms, racks, pipes, and containers on your patrol route. If anything slips, slides, twists, breaks, leaks, squeaks, sticks, sways, or smokes—and it is not supposed to—you immediately restrain it, repair it, and report it. By so doing you keep employees out of the hospital and your employer out of court.

You conduct such investigations as you are directed to conduct, or as become obviously your responsibility.

You act as a public relations representative, extending information, advice, and assistance to the public when asked and when it will not interfere with more pressing commitments. In other words, you do not stop giving artificial respiration to an accident victim to direct somebody to a restroom.

You assist the local police officers as requested in the control of public gatherings and the regulation of traffic; you direct and control traffic on the premises of your employer when that is among your duties.

You develop all possible sources of information to assist you (and to assist any legally appointed law enforcement officer) in the discharge of assigned duties, and you do not remain untouched, any more than any other lawman today, by the problems posed by juveniles, narcotics, permissiveness, strikes, demonstrations, illness, and accident.

You write reports regularly, probably daily. No matter what position you accept in security, reports will be required. If you cannot write a simple and accurate account of an incident you have observed, you must learn fast or abandon your interest in private security.

What is an "incident"? An incident, as the term is used in law enforcement, is any occurrence or happening which is not consistent with the purpose or routine operation of a business or facility, or with the usual activities or location of personnel. An incident can be an accident, a fire, lost or found property, stolen property, damaged property or goods, a fight, vandalism, suspected or attempted crime, or any other unusual action or condition.

There is no way to get away from writing reports and there is no way to exaggerate their importance. Talk to any experienced lawman and he will tell you that the success or failure of a prosecution often depends on the clarity and care with which an officer's record of an incident has been prepared. A report represents considerably more than a mere wish by your boss to know what you have been doing. Any report is just one part of a continuing diary of what has been happening on property for which he is responsible; what has occurred that is of interest to him, and what he should perhaps do, in view of your report, to avoid graver incidents. Report writing is not glamorous, it is not exciting, it is often a nuisance, it is often drudgery. It is always very important, however, because a report can be pure gold in bringing about a conviction or in establishing a pattern of operation which leads to an apprehension.

This chapter is not an exhaustive list of areas of private security employment, nor is it a collection of recommendations. It must not be inferred that only entities included in this chapter are considered worthy of mention, nor that the alphabetical sequence in which the entities appear has any secret meaning. One area of private security employment is not recommended above another area of private security employment, and the only thing that makes one more important than another to *you* is your own interest in it.

Armored Car Guard

There are a number of nation-wide organizations and many excellent locally owned armored car services which specialize in moving of money, jewels, documents, payrolls, securities, art objects, and other valuable freight. Guards in this kind of work do little patrolling, and the duties are predominantly in the areas of guarding and protecting.

Every move of such a guard, while he is on the job, is calculated and plotted. He knows, for example, when and in what relationship to other guards he leaves the armored vehicle, who remains inside the vehicle, what position he takes after leaving the car, how many paces he stands from the man next to him, and the sequence of reentering the vehicle.

All guards (three out of every four employees of such organizations work in the armored car or armed escort service) receive training in small arms marksmanship and thereafter are required to complete regularly and successfully a qualifying course.

Many men who are employed in this work have Army or police backgrounds, and frequently possess both. They are required to be in excellent health, are usually above average in muscular strength, are courageous, honest to a fault, and amazingly polite.

If this area of private security attracts you, be prepared to have your past life scrutinized coldly and impartially and in detailed chronological order from date of birth to date of application. You must agree to this systematic inquiry and be willing to accept the results. The investigation will be carried out through all sources available to the hiring organization including your credit ratings, and your police, educational, employment, medical, and Army records. Any questionable facts or information will be methodically probed by private investigators in the pay of the hiring organization.

If you are willing to undergo this sort of rigorous personal examination, knowing that every man leaves a trail a mile wide as he goes through life, and the thought of it does not bother you, you are probably going to be a successful applicant and will enjoy this work very much.

Bank Guard

Guarding banks is one of the security assignments in which, as in assignments to libraries, museums, and art galleries, the duties are perhaps weighed more toward public relations than protection.

Although, upon assignment, you will be told that your principal concern is the physical protection of the bank's premises, monies, securities, valuables, records, equipment, and personnel, you will quickly observe that a duty held nearly equal in importance is maintaining the best possible customer relations. There is nothing wrong with this. Good customer relations are important to any competitive business, and banking is highly competitive. Banks compete for available business on such even terms that sometimes the most noticeable difference between one bank and another is its treatment of its patrons—its courtesy and service and its attitude (as represented by its employees' attitude) toward its customers.

Members of the security force can contribute materially toward making a bank known for its good customer relations, and the appearance of the officer makes the first long-lasting impression. Usually your uniform is furnished by the bank. It is generally a conservative outfit, perhaps a dark blue fabric, medium-weight coat and trousers, white shirt, black tie, and a badge. A number of shirts are issued, and overcoats, raincoats, and rubbers or over-shoes are made available for those whose duties require such equipment. These items will be provided by the chief of security when you are hired. You will probably not be allowed to wear a bank-supplied uniform to your home. Not even a tie.

Most banks take care of the laundering and dry cleaning of uniforms. Soiled shirts, for example, will be laundered twice a week. Uniforms should be cleaned and pressed often enough to keep them looking their best, and should in no instance go with-out cleaning and pressing for more than ten days.

In communities that require licensing of guards, you will have to be licensed by the proper local authority, and it is likely that the badge issued by the licensing authority must be carried while you are on duty.

You will probably be armed while on duty but will not have permission or authority to go armed when not on duty. The bank will furnish your sidearm, fully loaded and holstered. It will be registered under its serial number and assigned to you. You may not ever exchange weapons with another guard. At the comple-tion of your day's work you will place your sidearm in the equip-ment and uniform locker which has been assigned to you. You will be held responsible for the cleanliness of your weapon at the periodic inspections held by the chief of security.

On the job you will be positioned at a "station" and must re-main there—alert, observant, aware—until you are either relieved by another guard or by orders from the chief of security. Under no circumstances will you leave your station without first notify-ing the chief of security. Unless otherwise instructed, you will re-main at your station when the holdup alarm sounds, ready for any emergency, until the cause of the alarm has been investigated by the chief of security.

If you are assigned to the first floor of a bank, you will prob-ably be required to stand throughout your tour of duty. On the first floor, and in such other areas as are designated, you may not smoke; in all other areas you will use discretion and good judg-ment as to when you may sit or smoke during duty hours.

Naturally, you will be expected to become familiar with the locations of fire-fighting equipment and fire alarm boxes.

Some confusion, leveling off now, entered the area of bank security procedures because of the Bank Protection Act of 1968, specifically *Title 12: Banks and Banking.*

Because of the rather general wording of some of the Title's sections (and also because there just were not enough professionals available), all sorts of persons, very few with any security knowledge or training, suddenly found themselves named "security officer" for their bank (in addition to their regular bank duties) and faced with responsibilities which they found strange and confusing.

These instant security officers were required to set up and administer a security program for the bank based on a timetable and nine minimal procedural requirements.

Because you as a bank security officer should be familiar with these minimal requirements, they are listed here:

1. A schedule must be established for, and a record kept of, the inspection, testing, and servicing of all security devices.

2. Currency must be kept at a reasonable minimum and a procedure provided for removing excess currency.

3. Currency at tellers' window must be kept at a reasonable minimum.

4. "Bait" money (used currency with serial numbers on record in the bank) must be included in the equipment of each teller's window.

5. Currency, negotiable securities, and so forth must be kept in a locked vault or safe during nonbusiness hours, opening the safe at the last practicable moment.

6. Wherever practical, it should be standard procedure for a designated person or persons to open and inspect the banking officers to ascertain that they are safe, before permitting other employees to enter.

7. One person should be designated to see that all security devices are turned on and are operating.

8. One person should be designated to see that all cur-

rency has been put away, and that all safes, vaults, doors, and windows are locked.

9. Employees are to be trained periodically in their responsibilities under this security program, and in their proper conduct during and after a robbery.

Your duties and responsibilities will be woven into this basic protective fabric.

It is of course necessary and important that you quickly learn to recognize the officers of the bank and where their desks are located, and the location of the various departments of the bank. If the bank where you work has no house directory, get (and carry until you know it by heart) a copy of the bank's Statement of Condition. This is a report which commonly lists all the officers, directors, and many departments of a bank.

Many questions will be directed to you and sometimes you may have to answer a question by asking a question. For example, if you are asked the location of the loan department, you know that in almost any bank there are several departments handling loans and it is necessary to find out whether your questioner is interested in installment loans, regular loans, real estate loans, automobile loans, or what. Ask the questions you need to ask, and if then you recognize that you do not know the answer, there are a number of things you can do: you can inquire of a bank officer within your station, you can use the telephone to call the information clerk, you can refer the inquirer to a bank officer or to the information desk.

Complaints you will get, and it is part of your job to listen to them with attention, not merely with tolerance. Let the complainer get the whole story out, without agreeing or disagreeing, without arguing, without taking sides. Your job is to listen, gravely and courteously. In many instances the complainer just wants to let someone know he is dissatisfied with some experience, or feels he has been ignored or mistreated.

When the story is ended, you may ask the complainer if he wants you to make a report, or if he would like to discuss it further himself with an officer of the bank. Many times the complainer will not want either; but if you think it is a legitimate complaint, you should make a point of reporting the matter, after the complainer is gone, to your supervisor or to the chief of security.

If there is ever an accident at your station or in your area, you should take all possible steps to make the injured or ill person as comfortable as possible and then contact the nearest bank officer or the chief of security. Let one of them take charge.

In the course of your work you will become acquainted with many of your bank's customers. While it is desirable to greet as many of them as possible by name, or at least with a smile or gesture that acknowledges their presence, you should not engage in any unnecessary conversation with them. You are a security officer, not a receptionist. That caution extends to conversations with other security officers or with other bank employees as well, and of course you will never discuss the operations of the protective system with unauthorized persons, nor answer questions about the bank's operations. All such inquiries should be referred to an officer of the bank.

Do not parcel out your courtesy or respect, or try to judge the importance of a customer by dress or general appearance. If a poorly dressed customer inquires about a loan, it is not to be assumed that the only kind of loan such a person would want is an installment loan. The inquirer may be negotiating to buy the building you are working in!

If you are not the chief of security you may feel that it is not your place to seek the acquaintance of local police officers. Maybe you are right, but maybe you are wrong. The law says that the bank security officer shall seek the advice of law enforcement officers, so even if you are the newest security officer on the bank's staff, no injury could possibly follow if you introduced yourself to the police officers on the beat. They are the friends you will be calling if anything develops that the security staff cannot handle. Do not hide from them.

Your job is complex because banks, just as any other building designed to serve the public, may not deny access to anyone who chooses to enter on business. Therefore, never fail to keep an observant eye on who comes in and who goes out; check the trash receptacles, washrooms, storage closets, and remote areas of the building carefully and regularly, and if there is no present examination of incoming package deliveries maybe you should suggest something of the sort. If, for some reason, the local police have not already done so.

Banks once had all the silent, remote sanctity of a cathedral. Today neither banks nor cathedrals are safe from the deranged and the vicious. Waste no time in inquiring with firm courtesy the business of any questionable character appearing in your area of responsibility. If the person does not seem to have immediate legitimate business to transact, either guide him quietly out of the bank or call the chief of security or the police because occasionally, although your job is ordinarily calm and peaceful, the atmosphere changes swiftly to menace.

There was the time, for example, that the coatless, hatless man in shabby shirt and trousers shoved his way to the head of the line at the sidewalk window of the Main Street Bank. No one within earshot understood his vague muttered phrases, but all saw him take a small, dark gun from his right-hand trouser pocket and hold it at his side, pointed toward the sidewalk. The woman who was first in line bravely told the teller to call the guard. The guard, on his arrival, approached the armed man goodhumoredly and led him to one side. The man still kept the gun pointed downward at the sidewalk. The teller called the police and when the officers arrived a few minutes later, the bank guard had the disturbed man some thirty feet away from the line at the teller's window and was still talking to him earnestly and seriously.

The guard had a right to feel pretty good about the quiet, prompt, restrained way he handled the situation. No screams, no panicky customers, no injuries, no holdup—no prosecution either, probably, for the man was an obvious mental case. Pretty good, indeed, but a narrow, narrow escape all the same. Anything could have happened. When the police officers, on their arrival, put the man up against the side of the building for a wall search, they removed from his person, in addition to the revolver he still held pointed toward the ground, one snubnose automatic, one derringer, one straight razor, one ice pick, one can of pepper, and one stick of dynamite.

Paragraphs ago it was said that you are a security officer, not a receptionist. Neither are you a doorman, an elevator starter, nor a traffic director, yet it is no more than simple ordinary courtesy to offer assistance to persons who appear to need it.

It will not cost you anything to help a confused or elderly or handicapped customer with a door or an automatic elevator or an escalator. It takes only a moment to keep traffic in tellers' lines moving smoothly by calling customers attention to shorter lines within the section. It does not demean you to inform waiting customers of certain windows open for deposits only or for cashing payroll checks, so do it. What is good for your employer is good for you.

And now to a final point: Does it not seem sensible to you to determine, as soon as possible after employment, whether you are indeed a security officer or whether you have been hired primarily as a receptionist or a doorman or whatever? This has nothing to do with the bank. The bank is free to hire the employees they need or prefer. Maybe it has nothing to do with you, if you do not really care what you do as long as you have a job and are called a security officer. But if you are really trying to be a security officer, and find that your employer prefers uniformed receptionists, or if you begin to suspect you are trying to provide security for a bank that considers the Bank Protection Act just another unwarranted government intrusion into an area of private business, a bank that remains unimpressed by the Federal Bureau of Investigation's statistics on climbing bank robbery and burglary incidents, because it cannot possibly happen here, should you perhaps look around for other employment? Surely you will never be a security officer where you are!

Beat Man

The beat man is the free lance of the security profession. He is a one-man security supplier, an independent individualist, and there are not as many today as there used to be. The competition from the security agencies is hot and heavy, and most former beat men are now working for the agencies.

Not all temperaments are suited to beat work, and not all personalities include the built-in self-starter that puts and keeps a beat man in business. A beat man needs to be a hustler from the start in order to sign to contracts the minimum number of customers necessary to qualify for a patrol license.

In some places a beat man can obtain a license if he brings to the proper local authority as few as five contracts signed by individuals or businesses that are willing to hire him and pay for his services. Ordinarily, however, a large number of contracts is required, especially in localities which insist that at least two-thirds of a beat security man's income derive from his contracts.

He has to hustle to retain his clients, who are constantly being approached by his competitors with offers—sound or bogus—of better or more frequent patrol service for the same price.

No more than any other security officer does the beat man get rich. He receives only a small weekly fee from each of his clients (usually businessmen and shopkeepers who simply want someone to inspect their property during the night to see that it is locked and not on fire) and for income like that who can do more than shake the doors of as many customers as he can accumulate?

Where he is part of the local security scene, the beat man is probably the security officer the police know best. They see him out there prowling the streets and alleys night after night and they know from his record of uninspired but reliable performance that he is a steady, dependable helper.

No man is more cooperative with the police officers than a security beat man. He is generally a very conscientious man and as often as not he will test all of the doors on his beat whether he has been paid to do so or not. Many times he is blessed by the officers in the area for bringing to their attention unsecured premises. Maybe the entry was criminal, maybe it was simply an end-of-the-day oversight by the owner, but the place was open and the beat man found it and hunted for an officer and reported his find.

Often the beat man's name is on the precinct callsheet with names of the watch officers, and he is expected to call in regularly to the desk sergeant just as they do. If he does not call in or answer the flash on the box, the sergeant immediately arranges to find him and get an explanation. The beat man might be sick or hurt, he might have been attacked, he might be asleep. These things the sergeant and the command officer want to know.

In areas with special problems—a housing project, for example, or a high-rise apartment, or a hospital or university complex— some beat security officers have been turning in superlative jobs. Hardly a week passes that the precinct commander does not get a call: "Captain, this is Ernie. I might have something for you." And in every instance the "something" is a prisoner or two, often with the recovered loot, the stolen automobile, the narcotics, the weapons used in the crime. And then the beat man goes with the assigned police officer to the station and helps in establishing the facts for the official report.

There is one aspect of beat patrol (or more accurately, the local control of beats) which you should know about if you are attracted to this sector of private security. You may be refused a patrol license not because of any flaw in yourself but because in some places there still exists the practice of permitting only one private patrolman, or one agency to operate within a specific area, or territory, or a number of square blocks in a community.

This practice is sometimes found in places where there is no central control or supervision of the local watchmen, and where the police chief or precinct commander supervises all security measures in his jurisdiction. Such a man has the last word in disposition of crime control resources in his bailiwick. He can thus limit security patrol personnel on the theory that he is thoroughly familiar with the physical layout of his jurisdiction and is best qualified to decide the amount of privately licensed patrol necessary to supplement his departmental efforts. An advantage claimed for such an arrangement is that the police officers know who has patrol rights in the locality and can quickly spot and investigate strangers.

Unfortunately this practice tends to build up in the favored person or agency a sense of personal possession of the "beat." Over a span of time the beat takes on the attributes of a piece of property which the "owner" may hold or reassign at his will. It can get to a point where only by "buying the book" (that is, assuming responsibility for service to the existing list of clients) from the "owner" can a different individual or agency enter the territory with security service.

At such a point free enterprise is dead in that region. The fact that the businesses or residents in the area may be dissatisfied with the performance of the "seller" (the previous beat man) and not at all happy with the "buyer" (the new beat man) makes no difference. The fact that they might strongly prefer their own choice, or choices, of security program or personnel carries no weight.

The claim that such restriction is necessary in order to maintain supervisory control has a hollow ring to the ears of security agencies and personnel. Newcomers to the private security scene are taking neither kindly nor silently to finding certain areas of their cities made, in effect, off limits to them.

Localities where this vested-interest concept has been allowed to evolve are (or may look forward to) facing some difficult days as security agencies and security officers multiply and ask why, when their fees and their services are so much more advantageous, they may not even approach customers in certain areas, let alone patrol there.

Under stress of such probing some city governments have changed or abandoned their vested interest concept; others continue to temporize and reap the inevitable warfare over rights to a beat. For example, Mr. Black and Mr. White, both employed for many years by the Atlas Protection Agency and assigned to a square mile area in Anycity, USA, together resigned from Atlas and formed their own company, the Zealous Watchman Service. They then applied to the licensing authority for patrol rights in the area where for many years they were assigned by their previous employers, Atlas Protection Agency. They based their application on the "rights" they had accumulated in their long-time patrol of the area.

However, in the meantime this former employer (Atlas Protection Agency) had sold out to a Mr. Gray who believed (or was allowed to believe) he was purchasing along with the agency, rights to certain beats in Anycity, among them the area formerly assigned to and patrolled for years by Mr. Black and Mr. White. Quite understandably, Mr. Gray wanted his "rights" respected and protected.

So now we have Messrs. Black and White, of the newly formed Zealous Watchman Service, and Mr. Gray, the new owner of Atlas

Protection Agency, both demanding that the licensing authority issue them exclusive patrol rights to the same beat area, with both claims based on long-time association with the area.

This sort of snarl exists today in more than one city. The instance cited has not been resolved and at present representatives of both agencies (Atlas and Zealous) patrol the beat. Furthermore, two business firms in the area have hired their own inside guards, and several others have defiantly selected still other agencies whose terms and personnel they prefer. Neither the agencies nor the clients have experienced any challenge by either of the original claimants or by the local licensing authority.

This probably represents the breakdown of the exclusionary "beat" system in this locality, but what about the locality where *you* want to work? Common sense hopes you will find the free enterprise system in use. If Officer A has a beat that he has patrolled for years, it is a fine thing. But if there is a shoe store right in the middle of his territory whose owner wants Officer B to handle his security, some thoughtful persons think that no licensing authority should be able to say to the owner, "Sorry, but since you are on Officer A's beat, you will have to accept security from Officer A or get none at all."

After all, how far is a licensing authority prepared to go, how far may it legally go, in defending and protecting a favored beat man or agency if a beat resident is dissatisfied? What kind of licensing authority would want to chance hearing a businessman say, "I did not want this beat man but you held him out as my salvation. He has not been my salvation; he has been one big fat problem and what are you going to do about it?"

It seems to some people that businessmen and residents of an area have the right to determine for themselves who they will pay for supplementary protective service, and that they should not be required by the arbitrary boundaries of a historical "beat" to accept the presence or service of an individual or organization repugnant to them.

This situation has been reported rather completely so that you will recognize it if you meet it. It is a mossy area of private security which endures from days that ought to be gone.

If the free enterprise approach is established policy where you plan to work, forget what you have just read. The question of who "owns" or is "entitled to" a sector or subdivision or a beat territory does not arise. Patrol privileges go automatically to the individual or agency offering the best grade of service at the best competitive price.

If, on the other hand, the vested interest concept is estabished, there may not be much you can do unless you decide to challenge it. If you challenge it, you will probably win at the end. But instead, why not consider, at least temporarily, some other area of private security?

Campus Security Officer

Colleges and universities must usually, almost of necessity, police themselves. Decentralized campuses, spread over thousands of acres, are becoming commonplace, and the bigger they get the more complex are the problems they breed.

Ordinarily the local police department has neither the equipment nor the manpower to take on supervision of a few thousand sprawling acres in addition to the city jurisdiction for which it is responsible. The criminal element knows this and has not been slow to grasp the resulting opportunity to steal from offices and student quarters and faculty residences, to beat, rob, molest, intimidate, wreck, burn.

Sprawling campuses, however, are only a contributing factor. A little thought will show that there is an immense potential for wrongdoing in the elements of any campus population.

First of all, any such group is composed chiefly of transients. Any loyalty these transients have, and often the amount is small enough, is reserved for their home towns. Secondly, they are experiencing (many for the first time) the exhilaration of freedom. Nobody can tell them when to go to bed, when to get up, when to study. In fact, they do not *have* to go to bed, or to get up, or study, or do anything they do not choose to do. They are *free*, a condition which their immature minds immediately translate into *irresponsible*. Thirdly, with the campus population constantly shifting and changing and coming and going, there is a total lack of the stabilizing influence of a set of neighborhood standards which become known and adopted. The standards of the city or town of which the college or university is a part simply do not penetrate, and so do not influence, the campus.

The problems which these conditions spawn tend to overwhelm the night watchmen who all too often are the only representatives of law and order on the campus. These men, well-intended but untrained and inexperienced, usually report to the superintendent of buildings, or to the chief custodian, or to the maintenance section, and frequently are faceless ciphers to the administrators and trustees.

Their natural enemies—the intruders, the vandals, the thieves, the dangerous and irresponsible members of certain student and faculty segments—have found that they could (at least up to a very short time ago) literally get away with murder on campus.

So if this is an area of security which interests you, let's talk about it—and you—for a while.

With the turmoil on many campuses today, the applicant for a campus security position needs to have among his qualifications a very clear idea of how he feels about races and groups other than his own. And at the same time he needs to have an equally clear idea of how he feels about respect for law, respect for rights and property of others, and respect for orderly existence on campus and off campus. This applies to all security applicants, but perhaps with special force to police officers who are moving from community police work to private security.

Any applicant who is a bit uncertain just where he stands on these matters is going to make a very poor risk as a campus security officer until he completes a scrupulous personal inventory. Since every such officer is going to be working in a very sensitive community which will be his home for at least eight hours a day, if he has any prejudices they will show us very soon.

No such officer dares get involved in the slightest measure with matters of race, color, creed, or national origin. He only dares get involved with individual people—students, nonstudents, teachers, parents, visitors, intruders.

On the one hand, he is dealing, often enough, with an immature group of individuals who are easily enraged at the vaguest imagined shadow of unfairness or injustice. Some members of the faculty are no great improvement over the nagging student, and will add to the officers' difficulties either through deliberate malice or through a profound and happy ignorance of what the officers are trying to do: protect the life and property of all persons within campus limits.

On the other hand, he is dealing with professional people— faculty, administrators, trustees—each of whom is a member of a minority (though not necessarily in the common current meaning given the word) and each of whom considers himself a special case, exempt from the rules which wisely govern everyone else. All these people incline to scream "harassment" at the top of their lungs if an officer so much as requests them to obey the regulations set out in the college catalog and in the visitors' guide.

There are going to be an increasing number of jobs in campus security, so if you are a white candidate for a position on a college or university security force, how do you feel about black students? Black security officers? Black bosses? Or brown ones? Or green ones? If you are a black candidate for a position on a campus security force how do you feel about white students? White security officers? White bosses? Or brown ones? Or green ones?

Do you have, or can you develop, the patience to deal good-humoredly and firmly with all the people who think they are entitled to special treatment? If you have any doubts about yourself and your reactions, be careful. You are seeking employment in a community where above-average intelligence is the rule. Tact and courtesy will be your big weapons in winning friends and support because you too will be a teacher by the force of your personal example and performance.

For example, some colleges make limited use of student patrols, paid and on a part-time basis. These student officers go unarmed, have no power of arrest, carry a walkie-talkie, and act as escorts and observers only. They act as escorts for students who may be concerned about passing through certain areas of the campus after nightfall; they will take a seat in a car on a parking lot and remain there quietly watching; they will act in matters of traffic control and regulation. Their assistance releases regular security officers to concentrate on campus areas where sidearms and the power of arrest may be more necessary. If the student auxiliary sees anything that appears to need the attention of a security officer, he makes his request via radio transceiver.

You may be assigned as teacher and adviser to such nonuniformed student security personnel. You may be assigned to traffic control—human, automobile, motorcycle, bicycle—or to ride ambulance, or to patrol, or to man a fixed post, or to assist in crowd control: either a good-natured football crowd or a crowd of hoodlum "protestors." You may be assigned to desk duty where you will handle all reports, requests for information, telephone calls, visitors, radio contacts.

You will be required to interest yourself in the security and control of all buildings comprising the educational complex.

If you take a job in campus security, you may expect to find all the ragtag band of prowlers and trouble-makers you knew in other places filtering into the campus to be the same nuisances they have always been wherever they appeared. There may well be sit-ins, destruction, and demonstrations in your future. Be aware that the borderline mental cases who generally lead these disruptive upheavals will show you no mercy. They will humiliate you and injure you without a second thought. You must recognize this fact and pray that you have a security chief who also recognizes it. If you find that the college or university you are considering as an employer does not have a reputation for backing its security staff, think a long time about concluding arrangements for employment there. Maybe you would be better off unemployed just a little longer than working for such an institution. After all you did not create, and you cannot end, the conditions which have contributed to present campus problems, many of which are the natural result of years of permissiveness, if not of outright encouragement, by administrators and faculty.

Because of what appears to be a rather disproportionate concern for the rights, as opposed to the responsibilities, of every malcontent in the neighborhood, student or not, some administrators manage to make the life of a campus security officer a continual frustration.

When the protective Big Brother attitude of university authorities acts to keep its own security staff at arms length in matters of disciplining or prosecuting campus lawbreakers, it is frustrating.

When a campus security organization has, in the span of one year, 112 criminal incidents involving nonstudent juveniles, each incident involving from one to twelve juveniles, and obtains a total of one single conviction (with sentence suspended and six months' probation imposed) , it is frustrating.

When a campus security organization has, in the span of one year, eighty criminal incidents involving students, with apprehensions in each incident by the security staff resulting in not one single instance of prosecution by the administration, it is frustrating.

The cloistered halls of learning today offer a security officer a look at illegal activities of almost infinite variety: liquor, firearms, dope, robbery, burglary, vandalism, theft, shoplifting, strong-arming, arson—they are all there. You will meet law enforcement problems that will call for all your resources of competence, tact, good judgment, patience, and courage. You will see suicide, violence, and murder directly traceable to drugs and narcotics introduced by the colonies of freaks that frequently ring a campus.

You will, with all security officers, endure the relentless and critical scrutiny of every person you meet, and you will be judged without recourse or compassion, and for good or ill, on the basis of your grooming, your bearing, your performance under pressure, and the reports of those who come into contact with you.

You will be immensely encouraged in your work if you can get your supervisor, whether he is the president of the university or the chief of security, to let you attend the meetings and seminars held regularly by groups of campus security officers. At such conferences you will be enormously cheered to find that you are not alone and that many other dedicated security officers are working toward solving the same problems you are facing. Best of all will be the realization that the local police department respects and appreciates what you are trying to do and is ready to help any time you ask.

Corporate Security Force Officer

Probably one of the best places for anyone seeking good training and good supervision is the guard force of a corporate or industrial entity. Such a guard unit is the enforcement arm of the company's security department which is responsible for overall policies and procedures covering such matters as employee investigation and clearance, supervision, disaster and emergency preparedness, inspection, education and training, complaints and allied security functions.

Many manufacturers have government contracts and are therefore obligated to comply with government requirements for protection of the plans embodied in the manufacturing contract. Often the almost military appearance, bearing, discipline, and supervision of such company security units results from this insistence by the government that comprehensive security measures be installed by companies holding government contracts.

Here, as everywhere, the details of your job will be set out by the company that employs you. The needs of specific industries cannot be described here because of their numberless variety. There are countless geographical layouts, internal and external restrictions, historical or preferred company practices and policies, security standards and requirements, so what is said here is in broad terms.

Corporate employers, when they accept you, often uniform and equip you right down to badge, nameplate, and whistle. You receive equipment also—ear muffs, overshoes, reflector-type traffic mittens—for the seasons and the jobs.

Here more than in many places you will find that study and application to duty are standard operating procedure and that error-free performance of your assigned security tasks is the goal pre-established for you when you are accepted for employment. Basic duties are unchanged: maintain order, protect life and property, enforce company regulations and the laws against felonies.

In time of war or international stress it is natural that the Federal statutes dealing with espionage and sabotage get a bigger share of the security officer's attention than would be true in times of peace. Espionage is the obtaining of information relating to the national defense with the intent or reason to believe that the information is to be used to harm the United States or for the advantage of a foreign nation. Sabotage is the intent to injure, interfere with, or obstruct the national defense of the United States. It includes willfully injuring or destroying any national defense material, national defense premises, or national defense utility; or willfully making or attempting to make in a defective manner, any defense material, or any tool, machine, implement, utensil, or receptacle used or employed in making, producing, manufacturing, or repairing any such national defense material.

Ordinarily you will receive a list of the regulations which have already been published and made clear to company employees as guides for their conduct. You will be required to comply with these rules and regulations yourself and there will be a certain number of them that you must enforce at all times without exception.

You will be expected to watch for fires, query suspicious persons, protect confidential aspects of your employer's affairs, guard classified material against loss, compromise (this means do not let any unauthorized person see it), theft, or damage.

You are usually responsible for the safety and behavior of the employees and visitors on the premises, and for the equipment, records, supplies, and property in your jurisdiction. You will be concerned with the control of entrances and exits; with the control of vehicular and pedestrian traffic moving into and out of the plant; with the maintenance, protection, and inspection of all fire fighting equipment to insure its availability and workability in event of need.

In and around plant property your authority to arrest and to search and seize is subject to local police controls. Authority in some measure you always have, but because of conflicting state, county, city and community regulations and ordinances, it varies. Find out what it is, and what its limits are, from the local police department or from your employer or employment supervisor.

You will be in constant daily contact with the employees. Do not make the mistake of thinking you can recognize all of them. In a large plant this is not possible. Therefore, halt and question any persons you observe wandering around, obtain satisfactory identification and then see that they get to, or return to, the place where they should be.

Problems of drinking and drugs on the job, and guns and knives carried into the plant will be among your problems—not merely alcohol and drugs and weapons brought in by employees on their persons, but such things kept within the plant and boot-legged on the premises. Under such conditions accidents and absenteeism rise, production and morale dip.

You will receive assistance on these problems from your super-visor, and usually you will receive either preassignment training or on-the-job training for specialized duties such as truck checking at delivery and collection points, badge and pass identification, trash and scrap detail, automotive repair, or whatever the assign-ment may be. You will usually have good supervision from season-ed supervisors who will be on hand or within call to help with any incident you do not know quite how to handle.

Do not be disappointed if you are a beginner in private secur-ity and such a guard unit will not accept your application. Very often only experienced security applicants are sought by such out-fits and you will be welcome only after you have learned your law enforcement basics over a number of years. In such an instance, and if you have set your heart on joining a particular industrial security force, there is only one thing for you to do: get out and acquire the experience you need.

Government Guard

As a government guard you will get training and supervision, and there exists for your guidance a wholly adequate manual of procedures which you will be expected to learn and to follow. If you want to work for the government as a security officer (or guard, as they are called), it is required by law that you be a veteran. You must, of course, be mentally and emotionally stable, a citizen of the United States, have reached your eighteenth birth-day, and be able to pass a physical examination given by a Federal medical officer. You will need vision correctable to 20/30 in the better eye, and you must be able to read—either with glasses or without them—printing the size of typewritten material. The ability to distinguish basic colors and to hear a conversational tone without the use of a hearing aid is necessary. You must, of course, expect to have your references investigated.

These standards should give no concern to any ordinarily healthy and intelligent applicant, who will receive consideration for employment without regard to race, religion, sex, national origin, political affiliation, or any other nonmerit factor.

It is possible to enter this area of government service without experience, but you must be willing to start at the lowest salary level. If you come in as a beginner, you will probably be required to pass a written test to prove your ability to understand written instructions and to follow spoken orders.

If you bring a background of experience, your beginning salary will be higher and you may not have to take the written test. What kind of experience? Service in the Armed Forces or coast guard which included or involved performance of security or guard duties on a regular or intermittent basis would be accepted. So would service in a public or private security organization or agency which protected lives and/or property against fire, theft, damage, accident, or trespass; and maintained law and order.

Government guards patrol all types of Federal properties throughout the United States to protect them, their contents, and their occupants. If you become a guard you will make your patrols as assigned, prevent unauthorized entry to restricted areas and unauthorized removal of property from all areas, maintain order on your post, control traffic, seek out and take immediate action against hazards which may cause damage or injury, enforce security regulations where they apply, enforce premises rules and regulations, make arrests for cause, make all required reports, perform such other duties as may be assigned.

The duties of these positions require moderate to great physical exertion and sometimes prolonged *courteous* contact with the public. Your normal work week will be comprised of forty hours; if you are required to work more than forty hours in an emergency, you will receive equal time off after the stress period passes.

Your hours will generally consist of five regular daily tours of duty of eight hours each on one of three reliefs: 8 A.M. to 4 P.M.; 4 P.M. to 12 midnight; 12 midnight to 8 A.M.

The above relief hours are subject to modification to meet the needs of the particular facility and, as in all security positions, your duty days will often include nights, weekends, and holidays.

You are likely to be the first to learn of stolen property, of lost or found articles, of ill or injured or deceased persons on government property who—along with their possessions—must be protected, of lost children, of storms, of trouble.

Much of your time may be spent in areas where you have frequent contacts with the public. You are expected to be consistently pleasant and courteous, and when it does not interfere with your protective functions, you may help visitors to locate specific employees or offices in the building, advise as to what areas may not be entered by the public, provide general information or direct the inquirer to where desired information may be obtained, and refer to your supervisor any inquiries you cannot answer or which involve the operations of any government agency.

To get such a job your first move should be to obtain a copy of a pamphlet published by the United States Civil Service Commission called *Working for the U.S.A.* It is full of helpful information about applying for a government job, what the government expects of employees, and what the employees get in return.

Among other items of information in the pamphlet, you will find a list of Job Information Centers, and you can locate the address of the one serving your state and write there, telephone there, or visit in person. You will find the Center a complete one-stop information bureau about Federal job opportunities in your area and in other sections of the country as well.

If you live in a small town, you can probably get most of your questions answered and obtain printed material at your post office. If you live in a larger community, you may have a Federal Job Information Center located there. You can look in the black and white pages of the telephone directory under *United States Government,* and find the heading *Civil Service Commission.* You may find listed a Regional Office, a Federal Job Information Center, and/or an Interagency Board of Examiners. Any such office should be able to provide answers to your questions and so supply whatever printed material you should have.

If all else fails, write to The Civil Service Commission, 1900 E Street N/W, Washington, D.C. 20415.

Hospital Security Officer

Viewed in the light of current security requirements, most hospitals are pitifully vulnerable. Even in a tranquil time many would by now be old, antiquated, obsolete; even in a tranquil time a bare handful would provide adequate protection for staff, patients, equipment, and premises in an emergency.

Hospitals are vulnerable for the same reason that any semi-public building is vulnerable today: with their countless unsupervised entrances and exits they were designed in another time for the convenience of a public that had more respect for the rights and property of others than is fashionable today. Now they are having to hire security officers, although in many instances with a niggardliness that guarantees they are wasting their money.

The basic qualifications for employment are the same as usual: citizen of the United States, at least twenty-one years of age, good moral character, ability to read and write the English language, physical capability of performing the duties of the position you seek, and meeting the residency requirements of the locality where you apply.

You will need the physical strength to stand at all times in full view while on duty, to patrol the long corridors and distant parking lots, to climb countless stairs, to control a violent patient, or to subdue a suspect resisting arrest.

You will need an even disposition and emotional stability so that, when a nurse walks up to you and says, "Take this bedpan to 606 and help clean up the mess in there," you can say, quietly and firmly, "I am on duty here as a security officer. You require a member of the custodial staff. I will call one for you."

There are many hospitals even today (and not just hospitals, but many businesses as well) where janitorial and other unskilled tasks (sweeping, mopping, shoveling, running the elevator, delivering oxygen, burning trash) are listed on the watchman's job description. In fact, if you are wise, you will obtain some clear information on this point during your first interview, because if you give an inch you will find yourself doing custodial chores 85 per cent of the time, and security duties 15 per cent of the time. These very hospitals (and businesses) generally have more than their share of security problems and cannot understand why.

You will need the ability to handle firearms. Unless you are assigned to duty at a mental hospital, you will probably be armed. You will be dealing with felony violations as well as misdemeanors, and felons do not have any mercy on an unarmed security officer. Damage to automobiles and thefts from them are nightly occurrences on hospital parking lots around the country. The sacking of the cafeteria vending machines; malicious smashing of light bulbs in corridors, stairways, and passages; purse snatching, and harassing of employees leaving at the end of the second and third shifts are also common events. In some hospital areas this alone is making the recruitment of employees all but impossible.

Theft of hospital supplies, drugs, and food; theft of personal property of employees and patients; the bringing of liquor to patients, and threats of bodily harm to attendants if they report such activities; the menacing of nurses and physicians by loud, boisterous, aggressive, obscene patients who have not been discharged by their doctors but are well enough to roam the hospital as troublemakers and thieves—all are daily occurrences.

Few hospitals can claim to be entirely free from such security problems, though the patterns and intensity of incidents may vary. In any hospital without adequate security the seeds of trouble exist.

In any hospital without adequate security all sorts of persons of no known business can roam at will through the halls and wards, creating disturbances, annoying patients, harassing staff. In some hospitals the stage has already been reached where, with all the unsavory characters wandering around, it is not safe to enter a washroom or a self-service elevator alone.

You already know the basic duty of a security officer, wherever he works: to patrol regularly for the purpose of protecting the premises and the building, together with their contents and occupants, given into his care. A hospital assignment is no different. You protect life and property, keep the peace, maintain order, prevent crime, watch for fire, enforce hospital rules and regulations, provide all required reports.

You are expected to assume responsibility for visitor control, premises protection, and fire watch. You are expected to patrol the floors of the various buildings which comprise the complex: the morgue, the loading dock, the laundry, the linen rooms, the kitchen area, the nurses' residence, the doctors' quarters, the parking lots, the carpenter shop, the gift shop, the laboratory, the pharmacy, the cafeteria, the food lockers, the storage areas, the patients'-property room, the wards, the outpatient clinic, the emergency receiving room, and the interior and exterior fire escapes.

If you are the only security officer on the payroll, this is an impossible task; if you are a member of a competent security staff you will be able to handle your share of the job well and with enjoyment.

In meeting their problems hospitals appear to be dividing into two major groups. In one group are the hospitals that reluctantly add one security officer to the staff and wonder why it makes no difference in their troubled situation. If you accept a security position with such a hospital, it can be a dismaying experience. To begin with, you will probably find yourself reporting to an assistant housekeeper who is also responsible for the custodial crew and the maintenance staff. Because you are dedicated to law enforcement, you try your best; but your efforts are canceled by an administration which will never prosecute the violators you pick up—not for theft, not for vandalism, not for pilferage, not for trespassing, not for anything. You continue your efforts and manage to get some physical controls installed, but it is all for nothing. There is nobody assigned to follow with daily inspections, so alarms are regularly neutralized and doors and windows are propped open with a two-by-four or a soda bottle or a roll of toilet tissue and thieves enter from outside to pick up the linens that have been stacked conveniently nearby by a dishonest employee. Working under such conditions will only spoil you; any experience you acquire will be second rate. It will make a watchman of you, not a security officer.

In the other group are the hospitals that are meeting their security problems head-on, with an adequate budget, professional guidance, administrative support, and a determination to back the security officers to the limit in a united effort to make their hospital what it should be: a peaceful haven for the ill, the injured, and the infirm. Employment as a security officer in such a hospital can be an inspiring experience. It will be a hospital with a modern approach to a modern problem, where the entire staff is being regularly indoctrinated in security practices and where the security force is alert, well equipped, and supervised by knowledgeable superiors. It will be a hospital where the administration backs its chief of security by demanding the name and working title of any employee who refuses to cooperate, and by prompt and widely publicized prosecution of any offender for a violation of law on the premises.

Instead of having to sign in and sign out at the telephone switchboard (and leave your revolver there when you are called to an area you may not enter armed) you will find that there is a guardhouse or headquarters for the security force. It may be no more than a room, but it is Headquarters: a place where the security officers relax, receive and leave messages, write reports, lock away equipment at the end of a watch; a place which, by its very existence recognizes and acknowledges the value of this unit of hospital operation.

Protection Agency Employee

As an employee of a protection agency or patrol service you will be assigned to one of the clients who has a contract with your employer for protection.

This gives you two bosses immediately. The client to whom you are assigned becomes your secondary employer and you must please this secondary employer in every legal way which does not conflict with instructions or policies or practices of your primary employer, the agency that signs your paycheck.

As an employee of a security contractor or a supplier of protection services you are obliged to accept whatever lawful assignment your employer gives you, and the purpose of your presence on a client's property is always the same: protection.

The hazards against which you protect your secondary employer—your boss's client—vary from place to place. In one part of a city burglary may be a major problem, in another part of a city vandalism may be a major problem, in a third part of a city theft from company premises (either theft from outside or pilferage from inside) may be a major problem.

Your employer will expect you to provide protection by observing and reporting unusual conditions and activities; by allowing only authorized persons on the premises (which will protect against damage suits from accidental injuries to unauthorized persons on the premises); by enforcing company rules and regulations, and obeying them yourself; by winning the trust and goodwill of employees, aiding employee-management relations thereby.

In some places—a library, for example—public relations may be a major part of the security job, while in other places—a pier or freight terminal, perhaps—the public relations aspect of the assignment may dwindle to the vanishing point. You may be stationed at a park, beach, riverfront, or other recreation area where, especially over long weekends and holidays, accidents and rowdyism may be your continuing concern.

In some assignments you come into contact only with the employees of an organization, and in such a place you will find that the public relations and the security are interwoven into a single unit of patience, good humor, and firm courtesy which you wear like a coat. If there is a union, you need to learn where your area of responsibility ends in matters of employee control, and where the union's area begins.

Watchmen, as such personnel have herein been described, seem to work in considerable numbers for protection suppliers. This is possibly the result of the acute shortage of security officers, added to the discovery by some suppliers that they can foist on tense and fearful clients nearly any borderline employee they have a uniform to almost fit. Protection suppliers are businessmen, and their agencies are businesses; businesses are not run by businessmen for love of the community. Businesses are run to make money, and more money can be made by assigning indifferent personnel than by assigning quality personnel. Quality personnel cost more, so why should any businessman cut his own profit by assigning quality officers to clients who do not know the difference?

In the mishandled situations which aggravate police departments, in the arbitrary and abrasive actions which alienate public sympathy, in the procedural blunders which are excused instead of disciplined, nine times out of ten the fault lies with the caliber of employee being hired and assigned.

Consider Jess A. Seipher: Jess's tour of duty at the neighborhood movie house ended each night at 11 P.M. On the night of the following incident Jess left the building promptly (in fact maybe a few minutes ahead of time) and went to the parking lot where two friends waited for him in a car. He climbed into the back seat and the three men started out.

Seipher should have been fired just for getting into that car. The driver was a man named Schlabbe, who had applied for a security officer's license and had been refused because he had been convicted of a felony. He'd killed his wife. The second man in the front seat was a known police character named Nosra. Naturally his nickname was Cosa, and he was the man invariably interviewed by the bomb and arson squad after any suspicious fire. Although Seipher had a driver's license in his possession, neither of the two men in the front seat had such a license. Neither did they have a registration for the car.

Barely five minutes away from the theatre parking lot, traveling east on a one-way eastbound street, they met a car moving at legal speed traveling west, the wrong way. A man was driving and there was a woman in the passenger seat beside him.

Unless he chose to call it to the attention of a police officer, this violation was none of Seipher's business. He was not on duty and the observed violation did not take place within his jurisdiction, but he could not resist the temptation to show off.

At Seipher's direction Schlabbe swung his car around in a tight U-turn and now both cars are moving west.

Seipher's car drew abreast of the other vehicle and, although he possessed no authority whatever to do so, the watchman signaled the driver of the other car to stop. The man, knowing only that three unknown males were trying to curb his car, put on a burst of speed, swung sharply around the next corner, and headed north at a high rate of speed in an attempt to escape.

Urged profanely on by Seipher, Schlabbe streaked in pursuit. Then, unbelievably, Seipher pulled out his revolver (which he was not legally permitted to carry off duty), leveled down on the car ahead, and squeezed the trigger.

A bullet smacked into the trunk of the lead car, which swayed to a halt with its nose well into the intersection of a main thoroughfare. A man stepped out, pressed down the lock, and slammed the door shut. Then he turned and leaned his back against it, hatless, white-faced, gray-haired, and breathing hard. He stared tormentedly at the three nondescript men who pulled to a stop and piled out of the pursuing car, and looked without hope at the gathering knot of watchers.

Seipher felt very important when he saw the man's Roman collar.

Later testimony showed that Seipher's prisoners were a Catholic priest, a teacher in an outstate college, who was bringing his niece, a student at the college, home to her father's house. A stranger unfamiliar with the local traffic flow, he had unintentionally begun moving in the wrong direction on a one-way street and was seeking a way off the route when he caught the eye of Seipher and his friends. These were the criminals Seipher proudly held for the police.

Two points must now be considered. The first is the outrageous behavior of the watchman who, off duty, away from the place of his assignment, and without authority to act, pursued and fired on a citizen for a misdemeanor which a police officer would have handled with polite restraint until he had all his facts, and which a seasoned security officer off duty would have deliberately failed to see.

The second point, of equal gravity, is the fact that the victims of this mindless performance thought that Seipher and his friends *were* the police. It was not until the arrival of a pair of competent, even-tempered officers that they began to realize they had been stopped by—as the priest later described it in a letter of bitter protest to the chief of police—"some anonymous subhumans in peaked caps waving guns."

Seipher was not unknown to the police officers, and they were as gentle and patient with his "criminals" as they could be. Nonetheless, everyone had to go to the district station and let the watch commander untangle the mess. Finally, a shaken priest and his niece were sent on their way, after a telephone call to a worried father explaining as well as possible what had happened. He was not booked on any traffic charge and was supplied with the address of the prosecuting attorney's office where he might press charges if he chose. Both the watch commander and Seipher knew that he would not. In common with too many people today, he had no faith in the police, the courts, or the law, and wanted only to get as far away from all such, and *stay* as far away, as possible.

What happened to Seipher? Oh, yes. Seipher was booked on charges of flourishing a dangerous and deadly weapon, assault with intent to do great bodily harm, riding in a stolen vehicle, discharging a firearm within the city limits, and conduct unbecoming a security officer. It was his first time in trouble, or at least the first time he had been caught, so he got a suspended sentence on the criminal charges. However, his license was revoked and he will not be able to obtain another in that city.

The cornerstones of good behavior for security officers have endured without change for many years. Offenses considered grave in such men a century ago—appearing for duty drunk or drinking on duty, overbearing or oppressive conduct or vile language, leaving an area of duty without proper relief, assuming police powers when off duty—are considered grave offenses in such men today. Seipher escaped lightly, although he feels persecuted and speaks of revenge.

Some guard and protection agencies are becoming fed up with the unending trouble caused by hiring and assigning this kind of person to perform security duties. Accepting temporarily the penalty of lost contracts, they are recruiting, and attracting, and hiring a significantly higher caliber of men and women. By their determined effort to eliminate inferior employees, they are taking a long stride toward the level of public confidence and trust the security profession, in general, fully merits.

If you have any choice, join an agency with such standards. The number of such quality companies is steadily increasing and that is where you belong—among the security officers, not among the counterfeits arrested for the possession and sale of drugs, not with watchmen caught asleep when they were being paid to stay awake, not with the trigger-happy and the lazy, the thieves and the louts.

Railroad Special Agent

An applicant seeking employment as a railroad officer (frequently called a special agent) will quite reasonable make application to the railroad nearest his place of residence.

The railroad police constitute what is probably the largest privately supported police force in the world, and their employment requirements are based on character, physical and moral courage, education, and good judgment.

Railroad police organizations are fundamentally similar in structure. There is a chief of railroad police responsible to the general manager. Under him are inspectors, captains, lieutenants, sergeants, and patrolmen.

Each railroad has its own standards. These vary somewhat; however, an applicant must generally be a citizen of the United States (a citizen of Canada, of course, for employment on Canadian railroads), and at least twenty-one years of age. He will be required to pass a physical examination by a physician appointed by the railroad.

As an applicant you will probably be required to take a written examination. Actually, you will be taking two written examinations because your completion of the formal employment application embraces a detailed review of your background, occupations, education, and experience. Your statements on your application will, of course, be carefully checked and your references and former employers will probably be contacted in person. You will be fingerprinted and photographed.

Railroads are very training-conscious, and if you are accepted, you will get training equal to any except perhaps that provided by a modern police department. Training a special agent to the point where he can be trusted to act independently and correctly requires several years and thousands of dollars. Naturally the training will be slanted toward the needs of the road employing you, but as you develop in your work, you will be given an opportunity to attend instruction sessions in all areas of railroad police activity: fingerprinting, crime detection by the most recently developed scientific methods, arrest procedures, care and use of firearms, juvenile delinquency.

You will need all the help you can get in that last area, because there seems to be something about railroad trains, yards, and equipment which tends to make some juveniles even more vicious nuisances than their generally unlovable average. Safe in the knowledge that the law says they are just little kids, though they stand six feet tall and weigh two hundred pounds, they trespass defiantly, grease tracks, pile obstructions on tracks, pull spikes, jam switches, set fires on trestles and in stations, burglarize and vandalize, throw rocks and shoot rifles at passing trains, and kill without thought. They cause untold heartache and financial loss, and they do these things without the slightest observable remorse for the often-tragic results.

It is an item of today's credo that a child can do no wrong, and despite legislation theoretically designed to help you control juvenile irresponsibility the little dears are going to give you a lot of trouble.

As a special agent your basic duties are the basic duties of all law enforcement officers: maintain law and order, protect life and property, prevent and detect crime, make arrests as necessary, secure witnesses, and safeguard evidence. You will walk many a daily mile in the discharge of these duties.

It is nearly impossible and entirely unnecessary to supply a list of all the tasks which may fall to your lot as a special agent. A few examples will suffice: You check incoming and outgoing trains; inspect the seals on loaded merchandise cars; are concerned with fire and safety hazards every moment of your duty tour; apprehend or suppress trespassing, illegal riding, and mischief; protect roundhouses, repair shops, and freight terminals; investigate claims resulting from loss or pilferage of shipments; patrol trains and way stations; investigate derailments or conditions which might result in derailments.

It is your duty to protect the property of your employer against carelessness, negligence, vandalism, damage, fire; to guard the freight, express, baggage, and mail traffic from theft and loss; to protect passengers against gamblers, pickpockets, thieves, and rowdies; to preserve order upon the premises and the trains of your employer; to suppress any disturbances that may arise; to uphold and enforce the law insofar as the company's interests may be involved; to conduct such investigations as the management may require.

In the discharge of your duties you are going to run up against the usual mixed bag of disorderly persons, drunks, gamblers, drug peddlers, pickpockets, purse snatchers, and all the miscellaneous human oddities from the petty nuisance to the outright maniac.

You will become acquainted with the police authorities in the territory to which you are assigned and will work cooperatively with them.

Usually you will be fully equipped at your employer's expense with badge, whistle, revolver, holster, handcuffs, nightstick, flashlight, cap-piece, notebook, and manual of operating instructions. On the other hand, you may find that you are required to provide some of these items yourself; if so, you will always retain them as your personal possessions. You must have items that meet with your employer's specifications even though you might have some definite alternate preference of your own.

Uniforms, when they are used, are usually purchased by the employee, usually through salary deductions. However, the majority of railroad police officers work in plain clothes, though this is a decision of the individual railroad employer.

Railroad police have long since outstripped any need to prove anything to anyone. The individual members make up a large, competent, professional law enforcement organization, and the organization itself has reached sturdy maturity. If you become a special agent, it will be a matter of pride to you to recall that such agents have been cooperating with the local police departments along the railroads' rights-of-way since the Civil War.

Indeed, there have been times enough that they brought the law to places where there was none and where there were no other police.

In the very nature of railroad operations this could scarcely fail to be, because so much of the property the agents had to protect was movable property. It passed on swift wheels from one state to another, one jurisdiction to another, one community to another across endless miles of trackless prairies, desolate countryside, wild water, and menacing mountains.

If you are accepted into this group, you will find them helpful and willing to be friendly, but do not be disquieted if you also find them reserved and inclined to caution until they know you quite well.

Like all professional lawmen, they are alive today because they early learned to be circumspect and wary.

Chapter Six

The Quiet Protectors: Women in Security

Come On In!

PRIVATE SECURITY is not solely muscle work, and women are needed in this field of employment more than seems generally realized.

Over and over, male security officers find themselves in situations (especially when dealing with the increasing number of women and children who deliberately or accidentally become law violators) for which they are neither trained nor fitted.

The women who are presently in private security, with the usual handful of notable exceptions, are not the sharpest in the world, and new blood is needed here as desperately as in the ranks of the male security officers.

Probably no thoughtful person would willingly return to the days when there were no policewomen, who have so often and so thoroughly proven their unique value.

Just as grievously today women are needed in the ranks of private security personnel, and the need seems no more clearly recognized than was the need for policewomen until the women themselves—by their courage, good humor, and dedication to orderly community life—established their place in law enforcement.

The role of the woman security officer in today's crime-control picture is in the realm of prevention rather than apprehension, though apprehension also occurs with regularity. In simplest terms, it works this way: When the police enter the picture it is usually after the fact. They are called in after the crime has been committed, the incident has occurred, the deed has been done. On the other hand, the security officer is seen, over and over for prolonged lengths of time, at a specific location. She is known to be on the job at a particular place and can be observed there for greater lengths of time than can a mobile police officer. Thus, the fact that she is so obviously keeping an eye on things tends to forestall or discourage lawbreakers. It is in this area of prevention that the woman security officer can make an immense contribution.

There is not a city in this country that cannot use every woman security officer it can obtain, if she has brains and energy and a willingness to turn her gifts to the unceasing battle against crime.

For years department stores have employed women in plain clothes for surveillance positions on the premises. Women have repeatedly proven their effectiveness in incidents involving children, delinquent or predelinquent women and girls who need a firm but friendly hand, and as supervisors and chaperones for public assemblies, dances, exhibits, sports events, conventions, and similar gatherings. Women security officers make attractive uniformed receptionists—with the power of the law behind them—at industrial plants, hospitals, and businesses employing chiefly women. They are often hired by mass transit corporations to patrol vehicles, terminals, and washrooms at the various stops. They are known to be conscientious and closemouthed in clerical and administrative posts in security agencies, and they perform competently in undercover assignments.

Yet despite the fact that the need exists, the opportunity exists, and many more women than ever before are today entering private security, all evidence seems to confirm that they are not yet being recruited aggressively nor, once enlisted, assigned to as wide a range of duties as they are fully capable of handling. Why is this? There are a number of reasons offered, none of them very convincing. One statement frequently heard is that the hiring and use of women in this field of work is a new concept for all except the largest suppliers of security personnel.

This, if true, is regrettable.

Female security officers should be a part of every protection agency's staff, including agencies of modest size. Jobs are opening for women in private security not only because of the specialized abilities women have and because of the increasing number of requests for their assignment, but also because the number of positions becoming available in security are not being filled by male applicants. Every modern agency is regularly receiving and answering inquiries about the competence of these quiet protectors, and about employment opportunities in this area of law enforcement.

The standards for women are high, and should be high, because—the same as with men—it is better to do without them in security positions than to hire semiliterates and dullards. However, the jobs are there, waiting for women to claim them.

Minimum standards for private security applicants vary from place to place, but they would not be considered difficult by the type of applicant that is being sought and welcomed.

General Requirements

A high school education is generally required and the minimum acceptable age is twenty-one years. These factors have combined to produce a third requirement that a woman applicant frequently encounters: the requirement that she have several years prior experience in some employment other than private security. The theory here is that a woman in security will be assigned to a post of some sensitivity, and that the additional polish and maturity she will bring to such assignments (after having had her rough edges smoothed away on someone else's payroll) will insure her fitness and adaptability.

The health requirements are substantially the same as those required for men: a general history of basically good health; good teeth, heart, and lungs; height and weight in reasonable proportion within the flexible range established by the licensing authority. You must have good eyesight but if you get that good eyesight by using glasses nobody is going to care. It is possible that a general physical examination will be required. In instances where the applicant is being screened for employment by a business organization that provides a physical examination as part of its hiring process, the bill will be assumed by that business; otherwise it is at the applicants expense.

No probationary period is presently required for men or women in private security.

Whatever has already been said in these pages about the appearance, responsibilities, authority, duties, behavior, and self-discipline of the men applies just as strongly—and maybe a bit more strongly—to women in security.

Service as a female security officer may indeed require an even greater dedication to the ideals of law enforcement than is required of a male security officer. Moreover, any woman entering the law enforcement field needs, perhaps more than most women, a sense of adventure and an optimistic and buoyant spirit, because often this is work that can grind a woman down if she thinks too much or too deeply about it.

An applicant may be married or single. A married woman should estimate carefully how much strain a job like this may put on her home responsibilities because of the erratic duty hours she will often have. Also, a change in her husband's work could easily require a move to a part of the country where there would be no opportunity for her to get such work, or there would be a discouraging residence requirement.

Since we are discussing drawbacks, she may have to supply her uniform and equipment: winter and summer weight clothing, pistol, holster bag, badge, memo pad, handcuffs. It is true, and should be remembered, that more of a woman officer's work is done in plain clothes (nonuniform apparel, soft clothes, street clothes, civilian clothes, whatever name you prefer) than is true of the male security officer.

An applicant is expected to know some first aid, the general geography of the area, and the elements of legal arrest. Most of this can be picked up on the job, but be sure the information you get is dependable!

You will be happier in this work if you are a patient person, with a sense of humor and the knack of getting along with the majority of the people you meet and work with. You do not have to love everybody, but you should have the life-saving ability to take people easily and as they are.

You will need, for example, the patience and good temper to carry you through the unpleasant experience of childish male jealousy which will attempt to discourage and belittle you as you seek to make your place on your merits. The same proportion of little men as opposed every effort of women to make for themselves a recognized place in police work may be depended upon to view the presence of women in security work with the same ignorant opposition. It would probably be hard to find in this modern world a sillier attitude, but do not be surprised when it shows up. Policewomen met and conquered this roadblock; women seeking a place in private security will meet it too and, hopefully, conquer it just as graciously.

With such a disposition you will have no difficulty in getting a security position and you will keep it as long as you want it.

What Is It Like?

If you enter this field of employment, you may depend on having a variety of duties and experiences, many of them at night. You may be sure of long hours and unending exposure to the mentally and morally sick, to the point where you forget that there are good, kind, gentle, compassionate people in the world.

You will be expected to know your city and you may be assigned by your employer to a movie theater, a public park, a dance hall, or a supermarket. You may be stationed at a bus terminal, a railroad station, an airport, or a school crossing. You may patrol the corridors of school buildings, charged with the protection of the younger children before and after school and at lunch time. You can be assigned to most of the places a male security officer can go, and to some he cannot. Except where the need for physical strength is a prime requirement for the job, you can be stationed almost anywhere.

You will develop sources of information which the local police officers may add to those they already possess. You provide additional protection for the property and the law-abiding citizens in the city.

The woman security officer is limited just as her opposite number is limited: she possesses her police powers only at the location of her assignment and during the hours of her duty. However, the powers she has within those limits are real, and she is often much better at preparing cases for court or at providing crisp, meaningful supplementary material for the formal police reports about an incident, than is her male counterpart.

Female security officers are presently in greatest demand in the larger cities and the more industrialized sections of the country. It is in the smaller cities, however, that they are most highly valued once they are employed and found competent. In such smaller communities they often find themselves doing social work as well as protective tasks, because the nearest social agency may be miles away.

It is never easy work and a woman often finds it hard to balance her life constantly on a narrow and treacherous tightrope where The Authority (the security officer) and The Problem (whatever it is) meet. It is a dilemma many women have solved successfully by taking private security work as secondary or part-time employment and enjoying it very much.

Meet Connie

Connie is thirty-one, looks about twenty, weighs ninety-five pounds wringing wet, is a slim brunette with an even-tempered disposition and the courage of a professional liontamer. She is a free-lance security officer, which allows her to pick and choose her assignments but does not guarantee they will be regular. She has been married three years and until they were engaged she did not tell her fiance how she earned her living.

After graduating from high school Connie spent three years in her father's law office and went into private security on her own the day she turned twenty-one. As she puts it: "I looked around at some of the women who were making it and I said to myself, 'Self, if *they* can do it, *we* can do it'."

She would not advise a woman to go into private security on her own unless the woman has enough money to see her through a difficult year or two of getting started or, of course, unless the woman has a steady job and breaks into security gradually on a part-time basis. It is necessary, Connie feels, to be able to say, and mean: *"Well, what if I don't do well right away? I'll find out about me and security and I won't have to give up eating; and who knows, everything may go well right from the start!"*

Connie believes that the life of a security officer has to grow attractive at its own pace. Enthusiasm for it cannot and will not be forced.

"It won't work out usually if you go into it as a last resort or on a grim-death basis. You use up too much energy that way."

She had a hard time getting bonded, because nobody would believe the reason the slip of a girl gave for wanting the bond. Finally she went to an insurance man who was a friend of her father's and he helped her get it. Her bond is payable to the city in the event any action of hers required such forfeiture, and she looks on the annual renewal fee as job insurance.

She had to get all her security training on the job and made plenty of mistakes while she was learning. She learned, incidentally, that employers are not always the souls of honor—she innocently did some illegal things while learning and did them with the knowledge and encouragement of her employers—for example, moving into the surveillance and investigative territory of the private detective and going armed twenty-four hours a day for years.

"What training I have I got for myself," she says. "I've taken all the self-defense courses for women that I can find, and all the adult education courses at the high school that I can attend. I've fired the standard revolver and rifle courses for both the city and the county police officers and did better than a lot of the men. Oh, and I'm teaching a course in self-defense for women. It is only two hours two nights a week, so it won't interfere with my other commitments; and it's six dollars an hour just for having fun and keeping in shape."

About the training given to new security officers she has no illusions: "I just do not think they are trained at all. Not like they should be for this kind of work. I was fortunate when I began, because my father was an attorney and I learned a lot from him."

She regrets the fact that security officers have no trade organization to establish standards for them, fight for them, instruct them, get a better pay scale for them, and improve their image. If you ask her why there is no such association she hesitates, and says, "I guess it's because nobody cares enough to get one started. They've always been too busy scrambling for contracts and fighting each other among themselves."

Connie is ambitious and would like to outgrow her one-woman status and hire some employees.

"I've been turned down for quite a few jobs I could have handled, because I'm not big enough. If you are a small business and go out and make sales calls cold, even on a customer you *know* has a problem you can control, they won't listen to you. They just tell you you aren't big enough. They've been brainwashed by advertisements. People who hire guard and security services have the idea that if they hire from a big company, they'll get better service, and they are so wrong!

"I had a chance just last week at a contract to supply security for twenty-four hours a day. I can't handle anything like that—not now, anyway. But if I hire anybody I'm going to try to hire policemen. Sometimes you can get them on secondary employment if their department permits. Sometimes they moonlight anyway. But they're the best. No training problems and they handle themselves professionally."

She knows that if she does take on police officers as employees, she is going to have to raise her rates well above the local level for security work. She feels, however, that the prestige and reputation she will gain from the officers' professional performance will ultimately pay off in more lucrative contracts.

"I'm in the business for just one thing: money," she says frankly. "But all the same, I think the reputation of all of us would benefit if we started paying better salaries and maybe taking a little less profit for a while. I would not work for two or three dollars an hour! I am *worth* more than that! I once was sent out with a man partner who was making just half what I was getting an hour. He would have flipped if he knew that. I don't see any reason for that sort of thing."

Connie works day or night, whatever the job calls for, seven watches a week, but limits herself to eight hours in each twenty-four. Since she works at a straight hourly rate, no matter when the hours come, she insists that the hours be consecutive.

"No three, three, and two, in twenty-four hours for this girl."

Since she is in business for herself, her rate is whatever she can get. "It all depends on how liberal I feel and how hard I have to work," she says.

She usually carries a small tape-recorder (always set at RECORD) in her purse, along with an ugly-looking little revolver, with which she can outshoot most of her male competitors. Along with most women security officers she has suffered the common and disheartening experience of being undeservedly blackguarded and downgraded by male officers.

"Sometimes I don't think it is worth all the grief and effort and then I snap out of the mood and get pluggin' again."

In the past year she has worked for, among other clients, a jeweler, a fur company, a supermarket which will pay her fifty dollars a day any day she wants to work, an insurance company, a bingo party where there was a grand prize of 2000 one-dollar bills on the table, and a department store.

She often works as an armed guard and the jeweler who employed her has a special place in her memory book.

"The assignment was to provide inconspicuous protection at a display of fashion jewelry at the Downtown Hotel. When I took the job he told me, 'Now, don't worry. There's no risk,' but there was nothing else all day. This display had been advertised in the papers real big and it was catered and there was all kinds of porters and waitresses in and out. It was supposed to be a private party but he didn't know *me* very well, when it comes to that. I earned my fee for that eight hours because let me tell you I worried about that jewelry all day long.

"I met the man at his office and walked him four or five blocks to the garage where he had his car, him with an attache case full of diamonds and whatever. He was so careless! He set the attache case down—of course, nobody knew what was in it, I hoped!—and left me with it while he went down to the lower level to get his car and then drove back to pick me up.

"We were told there would be only one entrance to the display room and that the back door would be locked as soon as we got in. Well, I checked the building back and front and found

at least ten unsecured windows anybody could come through and
no guard on back door or front door! We were there from eleven
o'clock in the morning until two o'clock in the afternoon before
the showing began. There were about two hundred women there,
and he's parceling out half-a-million dollars worth of jewelry to
models he never saw before!! One model was wearing a ring
valued at ten thousand dollars, wandering around among the
guests! They had to mingle with the guests and I'll bet you there
wasn't a minute I couldn't have walked out unnoticed with ten
thousand dollars worth of jewelry in my pocket.

"And then about four o'clock in the afternoon I got back into
his car with him and we drove downtown, and back to the garage,
and walked to his office, and up in the elevator. Yet you can't
tell these people anything. They get angry with you. They won't
call you any more."

On Connie's left wrist, angling up the back from the base of
her thumb, is a three-inch scar, still red—a souvenir of the department store assignment.

"A widdle kid gave me that," Connie will tell you, with an
engaging sourness, "and they didn't even book her."

The incident, or one like it, is repeated a hundred times a
week across the nation: About five o'clock one afternoon—a
Thursday, so the store would be open until nine o'clock in the
evening, Connie recalls—she was in the girls' clothing department
when she saw Norine prowling through the aisles. Connie knew
Norine well, since she had picked up the fourteen-year-old delinquent three times for shoplifting in the store. However, since no
prosecution ever took place, Norine reasonably began to figure
that shoplifting was just dandy with everybody except the gahdam
lady fuzz who was fixin' to get herself killed.

Norine's radar swiftly picked up Connie and she whirled
viciously on the officer, screaming, "Yuh stinkin' old bag, you
ain't gonna put me in no jail. I *kill* yuh first!"

Connie was on the shrieking teen-age vixen in a moment, and
pinned her flailing arms. She wrestled the girl to the automatic
elevator while store customers watched expressionlessly or turned
away. She punched the elevator button and looked with puzzled

surprise at the smear of blood she left on the panel. The elevator stopped with a load of shoppers. Some of them stepped out, looking with fear at the silent, struggling women. Connie maneuvered Norine through the door and into the car, panting, "You're under arrest. Peace disturbance. I'm *arresting* you, you *hear?*" Norine broke loose just as the door began to close, and slid through the narrowing opening quick as a greased snake, bumping her face on the rubber guard of the closing door. Reacting to the bump, the cab door reopened and Connie dove after her prisoner, nailed her, and finally brought her to the security office.

It was there that she realized her left hand was slippery with blood and she said, "Oh God, now what?" and, leaving her prisoner with the security chief, went to the washroom to see what had happened.

She turned the faucet full on into the face bowl and located the source of the bleeding as the rushing water foamed red and then pink and then swirled away. With her right hand she wadded some paper towels into a pad which she pressed firmly onto the gash. Then, holding the makeshift bandage tightly in place, she returned to the security office. She was standing that way when the police arrived.

Instantly, her voice shrill with hatred, Norine began shrieking charges: She hadn't done anything, but *them* two (pointing to the security chief and Connie) had questioned her about *nothing* and *then,* when she didn't answer immediately *she* [pointing to Connie] hit her in the face three times, inflicting a nose and lip injury.

Indeed, Norine's face had a puffy look, but it did not look nearly as bad as her juvenile record and the police placed no credence in her story, especially after a quick search turned up the razor blade she had used to slash Connie, *and* the two skirts she was wearing, the under one with the store's price tag still on it.

The store doctor attended both Connie and Norine while the police contacted Norine's mother, who declined to come to the police station to pick up her daughter.

The mother was told she would be notified when to bring her daughter for juvenile court appearance. Norine was escorted home in a squad car, and Connie went back to duty in her blood-stained dress until the security chief decided she was not improving the store's image and sent her home. Because of her age, Norine was not even booked.

"We'll probably wait until she kills somebody and then everyone will be surprised," Connie says, "but that's life."

There are not nearly enough Connies in private security. A lot more are needed, and the sooner they come along the better it will be for private security. They will give the profession a fine name and add enormously to its prestige.

III

THE FUTURE

Chapter Seven

Where the Action Is

A Giant Is Stirring

THE PROSPECT is not pleasing, but the persistent atmosphere of violence in which we are living seems likely to get worse before it gets better.

Pursuing this thought to its sorry limit, how remote then is the day when one half of this nation's population will be composed of criminals and the other half will be the targets of criminal seige?

It seems a fair statement that the police cannot much longer protect the public as the police would like to do, and continue at the same time to provide all the other services—the social work, the public health duties, the child guidance—the public insistently demands of them. At what point in such a situation may the thin blue line of protection provided by our police officers, already stretched to the danger point, possibly give way? If it does give way, where will the law-abiding turn? As we have seen, it is useless to look to the community for protection. The community cannot control the behavior of its members when the population grows beyond a few hundred.

There are few government units that have not, at one time or another, experimented with volunteer civilian groups as solutions for law enforcement problems. With no intended criticism of the goodwill or the good intentions of such volunteer groups, they have rarely failed to visit on the community more problems than they solved. Scarcely could it be otherwise. The complicated area of law enforcement and crime prevention is not proper territory for untrained citizens of good will to dabble in between 9 P.M. and midnight of a balmy spring evening. It is a social, emotional, and legal jungle wherein only professionals belong twenty-four hours a day, seven days a week, twelve months a year.

If that is admitted, must it not then be granted likely that in a climate of menace such as today shadows our happiest hours, no anticrime campaign will be as successful as it might be, so long as it disregards and excludes the trained private security officer? A lot of people are taking long appraising looks at privately licensed security officers. "Here," these people are saying thoughtfully to themselves, "we have a group of men and women who have learned, one way or another, some law enforcement basics. They know their part of town, they have been in this work long enough to be out of the amateur class, they have survived their baptism of fire, and they know arrest procedures right through the wording of the Miranda warnings."

Having followed the thought so far, a few ask themselves the next natural question, "Why, in this community's war against crime, do we neglect this ally, overlook this resource, ignore this combat veteran?"

Among the more obvious reasons, of course, is the fact that some people cannot forget that in other days such men have been used as strikebreakers, and as hooligan threats against business competitors. Other people dread an army of armed, privately paid, privately controlled patrolmen who appear to exercise fundamentally the same powers as do the most highly trained and experienced police officers while seemingly bound by few of the restrictions established for police officers. Still other people fear security officers for the bare fact of their existence. Such persons see in today's multiplicity of protection agencies dreadful evidence of national demoralization.

Such reactions are not valid, though people think they are. The employing of security officers as strikebreakers is outlawed, the times and places at which such officers possess police power are strictly regulated, and any irresponsibility on the part of a security officer can be ended in an instant by a report of the incident to the police department.

The present proliferation of security officers and suppliers of protective services is a response to a demand which is likely to persist for some time as an aspect of our daily life. Whatever the cause, greed and hatred and fear have grown too openly monstrous, and until they die—or at least until they are restrained better than they are today—we shall need and hire and use security officers.

The knowledgeable modern security officer provides for his employer a greater amount of safety and protection, and does it with less interference with the legitimate activities of the general public, than anybody in history except a well-trained, disciplined police officer.

He is emerging as perhaps the most important single supplementary crime-fighting asset of these beleaguered days.

Personnel Predicament

The number of men and women showing an interest in private security is growing daily, but too many potential officers are discouraged because of the persistent "watchman" image: the venerable pipe-smoker tilted back in his chair at the shop entrance in the setting sun of a summer evening, or sleepily at peace behind the basement boiler in winter time. It is a false image which persists despite the impressive crime fighting accomplishments of modern protection agencies and officers.

With all the vicious slanders spoken against all law enforcement personnel and the lack of understanding on the part of the general public, even enthusiastic candidates pause for some long thoughts about this lonely, thankless, dangerous life. Unfortunately there is very little aggressive constructive recruiting being done to counteract such negative influences. Very little money is being spent on recruiting, even by corporate entities that would benefit most from a roster of quality officers, and money must be spent to do a productive job.

Some of the best recruiting is being quietly accomplished today through the personal example of respected security officers whose work and demeanor has aroused neighborhood interest in private patrol. This, however, is not enough. Proper recruiting of quality security employees requires the full-time efforts of at least two competent security officers throughout the recruiting period. They would need to be men of topnotch appearance, armed with complete information about their profession and possessing some attractive printed material for distribution.

Any recruiter would have to be a man of good disposition because the instant he offers his story to the public he becomes a target for every complaint about every error that has ever been made in the neighborhood by any security officer since time began. It would be easy for a man in such a spot to become convinced that no security officer has at any time done anything right. Yet at that very moment, all across the nation, there are thousands and thousands of security men and women turning in steady, quiet, thorough, competent performances day and night without fanfare or credit.

Publicity is necessary to turn the spotlight of favorable public recognition on the accomplishments of these officers. It is completely impractical to wait for whatever crumbs may result from the routine daily news-gathering efforts of the local papers.

The one thing no recruiter may ever do is lower standards simply to enlist recruits. The last thing to be tolerated today is low standards for security personnel. A high price has already been paid, and continues to be paid, for employees like Billy Mac.

Billy Mac was no youngster when he decided he would be a security officer, and a casual municipal administration gave him a license and a badge when he filled out an application and attached the proper fee.

At two o'clock the following morning a police officer cruising the downtown area noticed an automobile with headlights blazing parked at an angle in the intersection of two main streets, requiring the occasional traffic to swerve widely around. The officer investigated and found Billy Mac in the car, drunk and talkative and with a loaded revolver on the seat beside him. The officer identified himself and asked for identification from Billy Mac, who offered not his security officer's badge, but a police officer's badge.

There are ordinances which make it unlawful to possess or display any badge or false credentials or perform any of the duties of a police officer unless you are an authorized police officer. No one may legally claim to be a police officer unless he is one; no one may legally claim to be a security officer unless he is one.

The badge Billy Mac offered carried the number 444. It is a number easily remembered, and the officer who was questioning Billy Mac had better cause than most to remember it. Badge 444 had been worn by his partner when both men were working out of the canine unit. The partner had been shot fatally in a street gunfight with an escaped convict who had killed the officer's dog and then turned his fire on the policemen. As his partner fell dead in the street beside the slain dog the officer now questioning Billy Mac shot the convict through the heart. The badge had been re-tired and was now—or should be—a part of a memorial to the murdered officer in the lobby of the police headquarters. So this early morning the officer carefully asked Billy Mac for his department serial number. The question did not bother Billy Mac.

"I'm a probationary," he said easily. "I haven't got one yet."

Hearing that, the questioning officer knew that he had cause for arrest. Police officers receive a department serial number when they are sworn in, and they do not go around carrying a dead officer's badge as identification.

Icily professional, the officer took possession of the badge, confiscated the car keys and the revolver, and radioed for a van. He placed Billy Mac under arrest for impersonating an officer, stealing under fifty dollars, DWI (driving while intoxicated) , and a few miscellaneous traffic violations. He experienced no trouble getting a warrant.

The stolen badge went back to its place on the memorial in headquarters lobby, from where Billy Mac had removed it in passing when he went there to take the security officer's oath and pick up his license.

Billy Mac is not, of course, a security officer now, nor was he ever really one in spirit. All the same, a betting man would wager that tonight Billy Mac is haunting the ramshackle taverns and dreary bars in some sad tag-end of town, carrying a loaded revolver and holding himself out as one.

In Union There Is ——?

Probably few fair-minded persons would take issue with a statement that security officers are underpaid for the duties and responsibilities they are charged with. Many of the very same persons, however, would take serious issue with a statement that the best way for security personnel to obtain an improved place in the labor market is through unionization and collective bargaining.

Police departments are split within their own ranks on this very question, and security officers may not anticipate any easier time.

The problem is explosive.

In the first place, security officers have no reason to believe, on the basis of the record to date, that their employers are likely voluntarily to change their long-time position. Management, while all but driving security personnel into the arms of union organizers, has continued to insist that private patrolmen have no right to form or join a union because their work requires them to remain neutral.

This song is the same one that management sang to the grandfathers of today's security officers. The theme is unchanged, the words are identical.

"You are a part of management [*but we're all full up in the executive suite*] and you have no right to join a union unless perhaps a company union which we can control [*for your own good, of course*] and if you do join a union, you are deliberately aligning yourself against your brother administrators [*who would not so much as put a padlock on a gate on your recommendation alone*]."

So the song is barely heard when unions say, directly and bluntly, "For years you have been forced to accept whatever they would pay you. Now we will help you to help yourself."

Management's retort "They'll help you to help *them* and nobody else" is not impressive in view of the fact that unionized security personnel appear to be the favored ones these days so far as income and fringe benefits are concerned.

There are, a growing number of people believe, certain benefits which should be enjoyed by all security officers. Benefits frequently listed include a paid vacation based on length of service, a guaranteed pension, overtime pay and shift differentials, company-paid medical and hospital care for the security officer and the members of his immediate family, group life insurance, company-paid holidays, uniform- and equipment-maintenance allowance, severance pay, paid leave for personal emergencies (*e.g.* a death in the family) and jury duty. These are commonly considered minimal, yet probably the majority of security officers would consider themselves fortunate to receive half these benefits. Many indeed receive none of them.

Inevitably, then, it must appear to the security officer that through unionization he can at last have a chance to protect himself and his family, to improve his condition, and to achieve the economic status which his contribution to the safety of his community has earned. On a number of occasions security officers have already used the strike successfully. Unionized, they struck as a union and tasted victory. Such victories quite naturally make a man partial to his union, which has done more for him than anyone else ever did, and make him perhaps a little casual toward outsiders, however "outsiders" may be defined.

Whether or not a lawman with such a tinge of bias is still a good lawman is not the question presently before the house. It is probably a question which, at the end, each man must answer for himself. Some men, in answering it, will arrive at the conclusion that it is a betrayal of trust; others, no less honorable, will decide that it is no more than healthy self-preservation.

Many potential union recruits feel uneasy about the aura of opportunism which seems to cling to some of the watchmen's groups, despite a loud social justice stance and beautiful brochures brimming with concern for the watchman. They recall union tendency to become immersed in politics at the local, county, state, and national levels, and while admitting that it is one of the ways to get things done, they cannot escape the impression that the leaders are concerned first of all with their own welfare.

Certainly it must be admitted that security personnel have not done very well in speaking for their own cause but they have remained admirably free of political and patronage involvements. The public is daily becoming more aware of the contributions to safety made by security officers and will not knowingly bar their way to merited growth and progress.

In impatient rebuttal many a security officer will say he is tired of waiting, that the public has not ever done very much to help feed his family, and that if union membership will bring even a little security for himself and those he is responsible for, just show an application blank! Such sentiments are widespread, shared by a growing company, and if employers of security personnel do not care for this attitude, or for the trend it reflects, they have no one to blame but themselves. For years they have exercised life-and-death control over the privately licensed officer in matters of assignments, wages, hours, and working conditions. For years the private officer has had two choices: he could take it, or he could leave it. Now he has another choice.

Tomorrow

What does the future hold for private security and its personnel? Prophecy is always risky, but the future seems bright.

Just as the war days highlighted problems of business and industrial security, the war against crime has highlighted problems of community and personal security. Private security is today a necessary law enforcement adjunct, essential to business, to industry, to individuals, to police departments. Private security today has the greatest opportunity in its history to become a recognized element in the nation's law enforcement structure.

The individual security officer has traveled a long distance from the bellman of the colonial period, and is moving steadily to higher levels of professional competence and public approval. More and more security officers are learning the difficult techniques of promoting and protecting personal freedom for law-abiding citizens while restricting and controlling the destructive activities of criminals. The best and most professional security officers aid rather than obstruct personal liberty within the framework of the laws they are required to support, and even the less capable among them protect many more persons than they bother.

Despite these facts the wholehearted public confidence and respect granted to recognized professionals has not yet been awarded these men and women. Professionals? Who is a professional? Maybe a security officer is a professional when the public says he is.

If this is so professionalism is today all but within the grasp of the modern security officer, but it can elude him. It can elude him if his employers do not care. It can elude him because he is not solely responsible for, and cannot alone correct, all the problems which beset his occupation. It can elude him because his widely advertised faults are insignificant when compared with the faults of many who manage, employ, hire, and control him.

Yet it would take very little to bring the dawn of a new day to everyone associated with this field of endeavor. A minimum of mutual effort, good will, concern, and assistance from those who respect these men and women, and those who benefit from their efforts and it is possible to foresee a day when the rule, rather than the exception, will be for political jurisdictions to concern themselves directly with the caliber, qualifications, licensing, training, and supervision of security personnel working as such within their boundaries.

It is equally possible to foresee a day when, to obtain any employment of consequence in private security, an applicant will be required (and assisted) to complete successfully a certain number of law enforcement courses. These courses will be completed within a specified period of time after employment, and the conditions will be a part of the employment contract.

Readers of this book could see the day when men and women who enforce laws have the same standing in the community as the men and women who make laws; when a descriptive and explanatory lecture or session about private security and privately licensed security officers is a part of every training schedule in every police academy and training center; when communication and cooperation between police and security officers are uniformly excellent. Security officers will routinely receive, for example, police lists of stolen vehicles, known and wanted criminals, thieves, shoplifters. Security officers see these offenders every day but, because of lack of information, often do not realize whom they are seeing.

Numerous committees are appointed each year to search out ways of controlling violence and reducing crime, and not one in a hundred includes a representative from a private security or patrol organization. Tomorrow will see representatives of security agencies on law enforcement and crime-control panels along with the delegates from the penitentiaries, reformatories, parole boards, welfare boards, mental health institutes, youth bureaus, legal aid societies, urban development authorities, drug and alcohol abuse clinics, newspapers, and all the others who make up the established cast of such assemblies.

Security agencies are often the suppliers of protection for certain buildings, locations, or facilities in a city, but how often are they represented on an advisory board? Tomorrow they will be regularly included at the meetings of various councils on community problems along with the members from the churches, schools, social agencies, and charitable organizations in the locality. They will routinely be invited to participate in discussions, debates, and community planning seminars dealing with law enforcement problems and community relations in the areas where they have personnel assigned.

Security officers today are frequently untrained or undertrained, but tomorrow could see allocation of tax money for the development of local or regional training centers for security officers, for equipment and supplies, for expansion of studies in the specialized field of private security, for the hiring and paying of instructors, for the defraying of costs for basic and in-service training.

The government's entry into the field of law enforcement education should reduce to a minimum discrimination against private security officers in matters of training and instruction. Loans and grants could be more freely available to qualified agencies and employers of security personnel for educational scholarships, and to eligible individual security officers for professional and scholastic advancement.

Business and industry will establish or support quality training courses for their security employees free of charge because no applicant of the caliber they want will seek employment where such training is not provided.

In short, it will be taken for granted that, whether private security is a profession or not, there must be no reason why its officers are not professional.

Tomorrow . . . .